Men,

Best wishes at have a met s. a . w !

D0873038

COPY!

The first
50 years of the
DOW JONES
NEWSPAPER FUND

by
Rick Kenney

On the Cover:

The Dow Jones Newspaper Fund has had four executive directors in its first 50 years. From right, they are: **Don Carter**, 1959-1961; **Paul Swensson**, 1961-1968; **Tom Engleman**, 1969-1992; **Rich Holden** 1992-present.

Praise of the Newspaper Fund
Over the Years

"Like many others who have chosen journalism as a career, I trace the beginnings of it to a Dow Jones Newspaper Fund internship. That was way back in the summer of 1963 working as an intern in San Francisco for *The Wall Street Journal*. After a 43-year career at the *Journal*, I'm still happy with that career choice, and still grateful to DJNF for giving me that early and exciting opportunity to report, write, edit and learn."

Peter R. Kann
Retired Chairman, Dow Jones & Co.
DJNF Intern, 1963

"I developed a lifelong appreciation of copy editors in 1970, thanks to the Newspaper Fund. For I joined the ranks of these unsung newspaper heroes after three weeks of 'basic training' at Temple University under drill instructor Ed Trayes. My reward: a Newspaper Fund internship on the copy desk of *The Wall Street Journal*, an experience I treasure to this day."

Jay R. Smith
Retired President, Cox Newspapers Inc.
DJNF Intern, 1970

"There ought to be a book – 'All I Really Need to Know I Learned in a Newspaper Fund Internship.' In one summer, I had the ecstasy of a Page One byline in *The Wall Street Journal* – and the agony of editing a mistake into an important story. Both experiences were invaluable."

James Willse
Editor, The Star-Ledger, Newark, NJ
DJNF Intern, 1965

"My Newspaper Fund experience has been one of those key turning points in my career that was the catalyst to so much of what happened next. I was able to learn as much from the formidable faculty at the University of Oklahoma's School of Journalism as from my fellow students. Specifically, I went to the University of Oklahoma knowing that my main interest was in visual journalism. One week into the program, I was convinced that it was the discipline to follow, a decision that has provided me with an incredibly rewarding and satisfying career, for which I will always be thankful."

Dr. Mario R. Garcia
CEO/Founder, Garcia Media
DJNF Scholarship Winner, 1968
DJNF Fellow, 1972

"I met Don Carter on the Haverford campus in the fall of 1960 and after hearing him speak, I applied for a Newspaper Fund scholarship – $500. He told me in the spring of 1961 that I would get the $500 if I could land my own internship. Two calls later I was in the news business. Had I not received the Newspaper Fund scholarship, I most probably would be practicing law instead of having a career in journalism."

Norman Pearlstine
Chief Content Officer, Bloomberg L.P.
DJNF Intern, 1961

CONTENTS

INTRODUCTION

Fifty years ago, America's newspapers faced a crisis of confidence about their ability to attract enough bright, young people to newsrooms. Journalism-school enrollments had fallen by almost a third from the record level of 1948. The Soviet Union's successful Sputnik launch in 1957 had sparked a drive for colleges and universities to turn out more engineers and scientists. For young people inclined to take up writing, the rise of the postwar consumer culture had energized Madison Avenue and was luring creative minds to higher-paying jobs in advertising and public relations. Television news was maturing, just as Edward R. Murrow was moving on, and its glamour was attracting new and talented journalists. How could newspapers possibly keep pace?

At *The Wall Street Journal*, which had risen to prominence a decade earlier, the late 1950s was a time of progress and prosperity. By Dow Jones & Co.'s 75th anniversary in 1957, the *Journal* was changing the definition of news. The architect was Bernard "Barney" Kilgore. Named managing editor in 1941 at the age of 32 and president of Dow Jones four years later, Kilgore guided the development of the modern *Journal*, which was the most widely distributed newspaper in America by his death in 1967.

In 1958, Kilgore and his top editors, with the financial wherewithal provided by strong profits, decided to confront the staffing crisis besetting newsrooms nationwide. Recognizing that journalistic talent needed to be nurtured in schools, Kilgore and the *Journal* launched a foundation dedicated to promoting journalism careers among high school and college students that endures to this day.

They named it, simply, The Newspaper Fund.

This is the story of the Dow Jones Newspaper Fund's first 50 years.

It is, like so many sagas of American journalism, a history of heroes, of great men and women and their deeds. The current executive editor of *The New York Times*, a former U.S. Attorney General, the most renowned newspaper designer in the world, a former Miss America and the former longtime chief executive officer of Dow Jones are among thousands of Newspaper Fund alumni. So are one-time deans of two of the nation's most prestigious journalism schools – the Graduate School of Journalism at Columbia University and the Medill School of Journalism at Northwestern University. So are the writers Joe McGinniss, Joe Eszterhas and Nicholas Gage. So are these female pioneers in journalism: Marty Claus, M.G. Lord and Karen House. And so are these pioneering journalists of color: Pamela Hollie, Ernest Tollerson, Wanda Lloyd and Juan Williams.

The story of the Newspaper Fund is also a history of high school journalism teachers who touched the future by passing on what they learned during summer study; of 20-year-old Ivy League students who competed for scholarships that supplemented their salaries as newspaper reporting interns and who later covered kings and combat and commanded newsrooms; of interns who participated in one progressive newsman's radical experiment that disproved a long-held, wrongheaded notion about what it took to be a copy editor; and of underprivileged teenagers taken under wing, their imagination inspired and their curiosity about the world channeled into the civic service that is the heart of journalistic excellence.

Eventually, its signature programs – internships, high school workshops and career literature – would touch hundreds of thousands of lives.

This book weaves together some of their stories, from the visionary Kilgore in 1958 to the interns of 2008: the life of the Newspaper Fund in its first half-century.

THE FOUNDING OF
THE FUND

By 1958, newspaper executives at *The Wall Street Journal* and many other U.S. newspapers were alarmed by the shrinking number of applicants for journalism jobs. Enrollment in the nation's journalism schools had declined by 30% during the previous decade. At *The New York Times*, Managing Editor Turner Catledge worried aloud that "the single greatest problem facing the newspapers today … is the problem of supply of human material." The talent pool, it seemed, was drying up.

Also worried was Barney Kilgore, chief executive of Dow Jones & Co., publisher of *The Wall Street Journal*. Kilgore believed that newspapers needed to attract and develop the brightest young minds. The previous year he had commissioned Prof. Alvin Austin, head of the University of North Dakota's journalism department, to survey newspaper recruitment and journalism education. Austin took a year's leave from his post to conduct the study.

His survey of 135 large and small daily papers disclosed that more than 67% considered "shortage of new manpower" a major problem. Pay for beginning reporters just out of college was rising rapidly, averaging about $73 weekly and ranging above $100. Slightly more than half of the newspapers surveyed were paying top experienced newsmen more than $10,000 annually. "Clearly, newspaper salaries have been improving faster than information about the gains has been getting around," Austin concluded.

His report held newspapers themselves responsible for not informing young people of opportunities. "To the extent that journalists have succeeded in tearing down the traditional stereotype of the hard-drinking, bullet-dodging star reporter (still purveyed by movies and television)," Austin wrote, "they seem to have left the wrong impression that newspapering is a dull and routine job."

Attracting bright minds, the report added,

> "is the newspaper industry's problem; many individual papers are tackling it with imagination and vigor. But it is also a problem of importance to the whole American society. Newspapers have always needed the best minds available to perform their vital task of keeping the public informed. Never has this been truer than now, a time of scientific, social and economic breakthrough."

Austin's study concluded that the greatest pool of talent was to be found on college and high school newspaper staffs. His report suggested that most student editors would welcome volunteer professional advice and that association with professionals might lead many young people into journalism.

Newspapers faced a quandary, Austin noted. Hiring was concentrated on college students, although impressions about careers were generally fixed in most young people's minds several years before they graduated from college. This meant, Austin suggested, that newspapers must capture the imagination of high school students. Especially glaring to Austin and others was the absence of "boy students," who had "largely abandoned" work on high school newspapers. He quoted approvingly the remark of one professional newspaperman: "High school boys are not convinced the profession is one with a future, and don't want to waste time on it. If we can convince them of its opportunities, they will return to the field."

Austin also surveyed libraries across America about their

vocational guidance material. One in New Hampshire illustrated the problem: Its books on newspaper work included a volume published in 1912; the newest was from 1940. Likewise, another of Austin's surveys found, school guidance counselors had journalistic career information that was wrong or, at best, unlikely to spark enthusiasm. For example, the Department of Labor had tabbed the newspaper business as a declining industry mainly because there were fewer dailies and weeklies in the 1950s than there were in the 1920s, although the Department of Commerce was listing newspapers among "growth industries," a rating justified by big increases in employees, payrolls and circulation.

One of Austin's survey questions focused on a debate that continues today among newspaper executives: Should the young person aiming at a news career go to journalism school? Of 128 managing editors surveyed, 91 responded that they would definitely hire journalism-school graduates ahead of general college grads; 29 favored the latter; eight expressed no preference.

Austin argued that the issue was less crucial than it might have seemed as most newspapers agreed that they wanted young people with a broad, liberal arts education, available in or out of journalism schools.

In any case, newspapers in 1958 couldn't fill their manpower needs solely from journalism schools. Austin concluded that newspapers needed to enlarge their recruitment from the staffs of college papers on campuses lacking formal journalism courses.

Some newspapers had initiated their own training programs for their news staffs. Austin's study disclosed 35 such programs in 28 states and the District of Columbia. Austin found that newspaper people believed there should be, as in professional baseball, a "farm" system in which rookies could be trained and exhibit their worth. A large-scale, formal internship program, perhaps.

Overall, Austin's study confirmed what Kilgore and his colleagues had feared: The stream of bright, young talent for newspapers had become a trickle. They had experienced the problem before. When a manpower shortage arose during World War II, Kilgore solicited from the deans of a dozen journalism schools the names of promising recent *female* graduates, who were offered jobs outright and trained to meet *Journal* standards. The "beauty chorus," as the staff nicknamed the distaff recruits, hit all the right notes. Yet after the war, women lost their jobs in the *Journal* newsroom, and staffing returned to the status quo.

By the late 1950s, Kilgore was taking the longer view. Major newspapers had the resources to identify and train emerging journalists, but smaller and midsized newspapers were hurting. Aside from university journalism schools and well-established college newspapers, there was no proving ground for young talent and no major program to help.

"There was a shortage of qualified young people entering our business," recalled William F. Kerby, who would eventually succeed Kilgore as chief executive of Dow Jones. "They were opting for other careers. We were concerned that newspaper work had become unfashionable."

Kilgore persuaded Dow Jones directors to form the Newspaper Fund and to contribute $80,000 in seed money. "We were beginning to enjoy some unaccustomed prosperity," Vermont Royster, who was then editor of *The Wall Street Journal*, recalled on the 25th anniversary of the Newspaper Fund in 1983. "Barney began to think about how we could contribute to the profession."

Kilgore wasn't sure at first how to spend the money, but he knew he wanted the company to contribute to the betterment of all newspapers. He sought input from his *Journal* colleagues, who fine-tuned their ideas for months. They convened for the first time at a lunch in December 1958 to consider how to proceed. Bill McSherry, who was Kilgore's personal secretary, recalled that he didn't know what to expect at that meeting. "Bring a notepad," Kilgore had told him. Around the table were Kilgore, Kerby, Royster, Robert Bottorff and Buren McCormack. The group comprised the leadership of the *Journal* and Dow Jones.

THE FOUNDING FATHERS

Kilgore was credited with having created the modern *Journal*, which passed one million in circulation before his death in 1967. He graduated Phi Beta Kappa from DePauw University in Greencastle, Ind., where he edited *The DePauw* student newspaper. A skilled debater in high school and as a college freshman, he was steered by fraternity brothers toward a position as a proofreader and copy editor on the campus newspaper.

He said later that he decided then and there on a journalism career. He also worked as editor of the college yearbook while remaining news editor of the paper. In an early demonstration of his persuasiveness, he convinced university officials that the dual assignment was such a great responsibility that he should be allowed to drive his Model T Ford – the only car on campus. He became editor of the school paper as a senior.

To obtain his first job after graduation, he used a key DePauw connection: Kenneth C. Hogate, an alumnus who was then vice president and general manager of *The Wall Street Journal*. Hogate hired Kilgore to start at the most inauspicious of times for Wall Street: the first week of September 1929, shortly before the stock market crashed.

Kilgore climbed quickly at the *Journal*. After working two weeks in the stock ticker room, where he monitored the Dow Jones News Service (widely known as the ticker) against a competing wire service, he moved to the copy desk. Three months later, he went to work in the *Journal's* Pacific Coast office and became news editor of that edition. He began writing a column and was brought back to New York three years later.

President Franklin D. Roosevelt took notice of his work and, soon, so did other journalists. Kilgore's reputation continued to grow during a five-year stint as Washington bureau chief. In 1941 he was in New York again – this time as managing editor. He revamped the front page and pushed for more interpretive and analytical treatment of business and economic news.

The following year he was elected vice president of the company. When Hogate died three years later, Kilgore became publisher of the *Journal*. He was just 36 at the time and remained focused on editorial operations.

Now, in 1958, his ideas about how to invigorate the newsroom and infuse it with youthful talent began to simmer. His colleagues at lunch that day in December included those whom Royster would later recall as "that little band who made the modern *Wall Street Journal*."

Royster had already made a name for himself, winning a

14

Pulitzer Prize in 1953 for editorial writing. Although he retired early at 56 to take an endowed professorship in journalism at the University of North Carolina in 1971, he remained a *Journal* contributing editor, writing a column and winning a second Pulitzer Prize in 1984 for commentary. He was appointed editor emeritus in 1993 and died in 1996, one of the most celebrated *Journal* writers.

Kerby's career with Dow Jones nearly coincided with Kilgore's but lasted a decade beyond Kilgore's death. Kerby had accepted a job at the *Journal* in 1930, right out of the University of Michigan, where he was Phi Beta Kappa. But when he arrived in Washington Dow Jones had eliminated the job because of the Depression. Kerby made it to the *Journal* in 1933 but left two years later when, newly married, he couldn't obtain a raise. Better paid but unhappy in public relations, he returned to the paper in 1938 and by 1943 had risen to managing editor. By 1958, he was vice president and editorial director of all Dow Jones publications. In 1966, he would succeed Kilgore, who was too ill with cancer to run the company. Kerby was a force at the *Journal* for 45 years.

Bob Bottorff, like Kilgore, was a DePauw graduate, and Kilgore hired him as a reporter right out of school. Kilgore summoned Bottorff from the Chicago office in late 1954 and made him managing editor. Bottorff was regarded as blunt and abrasive, someone who could lift the paper to another level, more suited to executive decision-making than to working alongside reporters and editors. So in early 1957, Kilgore and Kerby replaced Bottorff as managing editor with Warren Phillips, who had been managing editor in Chicago, and gave Bottorff the executive editor position.

Buren McCormack, another DePauw alumnus whom Hogate had recruited to the *Journal* out of school, had become managing editor in 1946. By some accounts, McCormack pleased Kilgore with his loyalty and sharp-eyed editing – nitpicking, as some of the staff called it.

After four years, Kilgore moved McCormack to the editorial page as senior associate editor under Bill Grimes. Neither Grimes nor Royster liked the idea, and Royster grumbled about leaving. To solve matters and keep the peace, Kilgore appointed McCormack executive editor when Kerby was promoted in June 1951 to vice president of Dow Jones. McCormack succeeded Kerby as treasurer in 1955. But it wasn't until McCormack's appointment as business manager of the *Journal* that he found his niche. He was charged with research and reorganization of the paper's production department. He thrived, retiring as general manager in 1970.

In 1958, then, the *Journal's* masthead listed Kilgore, president and chief executive; Kerby, vice president and editorial director; McCormack, business manager; Bottorff, executive editor; Royster, editor; and William H. Grimes, vice president and contributing editor. These men, except for Grimes, who had retired to Florida after a heart attack, sat down to lunch in December to develop their ideas for recruiting and training future generations of journalists.

"They were talking about how they wanted to become 'the dean' of some school," recalled McSherry, Kilgore's personal secretary.

That "school" would be the Newspaper Fund, a name chosen specifically for its blandness because its directors did not want it to be seen as a promotional arm of Dow Jones.

A FOUNDATION FOR JOURNALISM

There was a strong bent for schooling the next generation of newspapermen. They considered giving financial support for continuing education for journalists and to colleges and universities to improve their journalism programs. Since existing organizations were already providing some of this help, the Dow Jones executives decided to look for new ways to contribute to the future of journalism. "Barney said we ought to do something to change the perception of our business," Kerby recalled. "He suggested a foundation. As in so many other ways, he was right."

The executives decided to establish a foundation, with Kilgore as president and Bottorff as secretary. An initial budget of $80,000 was committed for 1959 to fund summer fellowships for high school journalism teachers and publications advisers. Kilgore instructed McSherry to "take it from here."

McSherry wrote a news release announcing the creation of the Newspaper Fund and the availability of the fellowships and sent it to *The New York Times*, the Associated Press and some other newspapers. He also created an application form for anyone interested in summer study.

One thing that separated the Newspaper Fund from other foundations was Kilgore's idea to focus on younger people – bright high school students, who might be persuaded to consider journalism as a career before they got sidetracked by other interests.

The best way to reach these students was through their teachers, especially high school newspaper advisers. They were the people most likely to influence the students; yet, most of these teachers knew little about teaching journalism or career opportunities in the field. Prof. Austin's study had found that high school students were being advised not to go into journalism because educators "didn't know a damn thing about newspapers," Royster said.

McSherry recalled that Kilgore "was telling us about some schools where the gym teacher was the newspaper adviser, how a lot of the bright kids just weren't interested in getting involved." It was common in those days for a school to put an English teacher in charge of the student newspaper, but that didn't mollify the news executives. "English teachers don't know too much about our profession," Royster recalled. "We decided to set them straight."

"Literature about careers in journalism was also in short supply," Kerby had noted. "The only guide we could find was written in 1914 and issued by the government. It reported that the average salary for a newspaperman was $14.50 a week."

So, the Newspaper Fund's first project was to produce a book about journalism careers for high school libraries, where students could read it and find inspiration and encouragement. Created by Kilgore and Henry Gemmill, a former *Journal* managing editor, the book consisted of articles written by 18 journalists. It was an overwhelming success.

BARNEY'S BLUE BOOK

Do You Belong in Journalism? was published in 1959 by Appleton-

Century-Crofts Inc. The book was slickly illustrated, from its indigo cover dominated by a large black-and-white photograph depicting the bustle of a newsroom to its pages of portraits of professionals and action shots of journalism. The Newspaper Fund offered one free copy to every high school that requested it, and more than 7,100 did that first year. Some newspapers bought copies to distribute to their hometown schools.

The essays provided first-hand, down-to-earth advice. Top journalists from newspapers as disparate as *The Wall Street Journal* and *The Rock County Star* of Luverne, Minn., offered their views about the profession and about a young person's chances of entering it. Readers were encouraged to read and gain practical experience through their local paper. There were essays about the characteristics that defined good journalists: curiosity, sensitivity, ability to solve problems and collegiality.

One chapter was a "picture story" titled "Newspaper People at Work." It showed journalists toiling: a pack of Washington correspondents listening to a White House announcement; a couple of foreign correspondents talking with a produce vendor in a Moscow open-air market; a photographer shooting a car wreck; a labor reporter interviewing construction workers; a pensive, pipe-smoking, pencil-wielding editor conjuring a headline; and the perfunctory picture of a coiffed and well-dressed female reporter "covering the women's world."

Perhaps the "best read" in the book was a tongue-in-cheek essay by James Kilpatrick, then editor of the *Richmond News Leader.* The piece was titled "For Men Who Can't Do Anything Else!" and Kilpatrick meant it. He described journalism not as a job but as a calling. Men – and, back in those days, Kilpatrick really meant men – who could even consider another line of work ought to pursue that instead. He wrote vividly about the pains and pangs of trying to derive a life, let alone a livelihood, from this profession ("… going to the office with a bellyache, wondering why the children keep wearing out their Keds so fast … asking questions, getting answers, not getting answers, going to look for the answers, not finding the answers, making do with what you've got … grousing at the city desk, swearing at the proof room … beating the opposition, explaining why you didn't beat the opposition…").

After all that, Kilpatrick concluded, "It's a wonderful life." He advised "talented young men" to "pick out an excellent liberal arts college, blessed by a few crack men in English, philosophy, history and literature." In Kilpatrick's ideal academic world, this young man would go through this curriculum for three years, then spend a year in law school and "try to work things so that he emerges with an A.B. degree."

Then, in a patch of purple prose startlingly misogynistic even for the times, Kilpatrick urged in his final paragraph that women perish the thought of entering journalism.

"If this were a girl inquiring about a newspaper career? I would tell her to go study nursing, modeling, the techniques of singing contralto, the making of spaghetti sauce, and the breast feeding of infants, all of which women do better than men. I have known maybe a dozen good newspaperwomen; the rest have been ornamental hacks, and sometimes not even ornamental."

More graceful was an essay by Barry Bingham, owner of the *Courier-Journal* in Louisville. "A Woman Has to Be More Talented, More Skillful, and More Determined," still devoted 10 of its 12 paragraphs to advice for boys. The final two paragraphs were meant to encourage girls. Bingham wrote, "I think a woman can find every bit as rewarding a life in journalism as a man can." But Bingham meant a woman could succeed "if she is willing to make a career in the handling of women's news." The opportunities for women just weren't equal to those for men, he wrote.

Thus did the first Newspaper Fund project come to fruition. But it was only a start. If education was to be the key, more had to be done to educate the educators.

The Newspaper Fund's board of directors decided to offer fellowships of up to $1,000 to inexperienced high school newspaper advisers interested in spending a summer learning about journalism. The board's proposed experiment seemed necessary and sound. But the Newspaper Fund needed someone with the journalistic credentials to carry out its plans. "So now we had an idea but no program," Royster recalled. "What we needed was a director who could pull it together."

Enter Don E. Carter, the original "Man from Plains" and a well-respected Georgia newspaperman.

2

DON CARTER:
THE FIRST SCHOOLMASTER

Don Carter came to the Newspaper Fund as executive director in early 1959, and in his two-and-a-half years he launched and oversaw several initiatives that served to educate thousands of journalism students and their teachers.

Like his younger cousin, Jimmy, Carter was a native of Plains, Ga. He was a graduate of the University of Georgia, where he was editor of *The Red & Black* student newspaper and was elected to Phi Beta Kappa. His early newspaper experience was with daily and weekly newspapers in south Georgia. After graduating from college, he joined *The Atlanta Journal*, rising to the post of city editor.

Carter made a name for himself in the industry with his ideas about newsroom recruiting and management.

He taught journalism in the evenings at the then Georgia State College in Atlanta and, as president of the Atlanta professional chapter of Sigma Delta Chi, the national journalism fraternity, he developed a "careers in journalism" program. He was a popular speaker and guest discussion leader at meetings and seminars sponsored by the American Press Institute on topics of recruitment and leadership.

Barney Kilgore was among those who had taken note of him as a sharp, up-and-coming news executive. Carter had been city editor for eight years when Kilgore summoned the gentleman from Georgia to New York.

In a 2007 interview, Carter recalled vividly his recruitment and ambitions at the time. "This was *The Wall Street Journal*," he said. "Now, I was the city editor of *The Atlanta Journal*, quite a difference, but it was a very busy time for news in the South, and especially in Atlanta. It was a good job. But the allure of going to work for these top news executives at *The Wall Street Journal* was greater."

What Kilgore had in mind for Carter for the short term, though, was something other than newspapering. He needed Carter's expertise for working with young talent. The offer was for a position with the Newspaper Fund. At the start he worked in the newsroom, in a corner of the reference library – "with the librarian staring at me from time to time, trying to figure out what I was doing."

"I was hired to be a one-man operation," Carter said. "They gave me a desk in the newsroom, and all these people would come by and look and wonder what I was doing. I wasn't always so sure myself. But when I got to work there, they had plenty for me to do."

The teaching fellowship applications Bill McSherry had sent out were already coming back and piling up. "[Bob] Bottorff came in to the office one morning and saw the applications I'd sorted out alphabetically on a long table," McSherry recalled. "He couldn't believe how many we'd gotten. Kilgore was pleasantly surprised, too."

Photographs from 1959 show Carter at his desk, wearing shirtsleeves and a bow tie and hefting a stack of applications about two feet high. He asked for and was quickly given an aide from the *Journal's* secretarial pool.

In the Newspaper Fund's second year, Carter got an assistant. "There had to be some sort of additional help," Carter recalled.

"I was trying to go heavily into the internships in the second year. I was told I could get an assistant. We put an ad in *The Wall Street Journal* advertising for the kind of person we want."

Patrick Kennedy, fresh out of Pennsylvania State University, applied and was hired. "One of his professors at Penn State saw the ad and recognized this young man as being ideal for the job," Carter recalled. "He did it very well." Kennedy's first major assignment was to help Carter start the monthly *Newsletter* for Newspaper Fund teacher-fellows. Kennedy also helped with applications for the second year of summer teaching fellowships and the first year of reporting internships. The mail in the tiny Newspaper Fund office was piling up.

THE FIRST FUND FELLOWS

In 1958, Dow Jones announced plans to fund fellowships of up to $1,000 for 25 high school journalism teachers who wanted to learn more about the profession. Notice went out with an application deadline of April 1, 1959, and a return address to Bottorff, who was secretary of the Newspaper Fund.

The company, Carter recalled, had hoped for a hundred applications, from which he would choose the 25 best. By deadline, 476 applications had been received in Room 2700 at 48 Wall Street. Screening them was a "mammoth but exhilarating task," Carter said.

Carter recommended to the directors that 131 applicants from 42 states be funded. Kilgore told him to underwrite the whole lot and to disregard the $80,000 bottom line. "It was a high moment," Carter said. "This generosity set an early tone for the long-range development of our program."

To elevate the program's profile and increase visibility, he sent each successful applicant a telegram at work during school hours. "These telegrams would be received at the central office of the teacher's school," Carter said. "And the principals would make the announcement, to much fanfare." Local newspapers usually carried a story prompted by a Newspaper Fund press release about the teacher's award.

The fellowship winners were directed to select any college

where a full and acceptable course of journalism was offered for summer study. They were allotted funds for tuition, room and board, fees and incidental expenses. Although most of the teacher-fellows found courses nearby, the Newspaper Fund also covered some fellows' traveling expenses.

In 1959, Carter visited 34 universities and colleges, talked with 94 of the fellowships recipients and conferred with deans who supervised the summer work of 18 others. He found the fellows "hungry for journalistic knowledge, anxious to learn, and appreciative."

As a result, many of the colleges began to develop special summer offerings that would appeal to these early Newspaper Fund fellows. Carter's encounters confirmed the Newspaper Fund's fears that many had been given high school newspaper responsibilities without previous experience or training. The Newspaper Fund had found an essential purpose.

In the fellows' reports, one teacher praised the Newspaper Fund "for pioneering in a field neglected so long." Another wrote, "I, for one, am now informed and enthusiastic." And one confessed to having had "a very erroneous notion of the work behind the publishing of a good newspaper" and echoed the Newspaper Fund's fundamental concern in posing the question, "If teachers do not have a proper appreciation of journalism, and I know I didn't, how can they ever direct talented youth toward this career?" Another report included this hopeful comment: "I know that with my increased understanding and appreciation of journalism as a career, I will exert every effort to guide gifted people into this field of endeavor."

In its first year, the Newspaper Fund's effort was producing results. One teacher in Houston devised an outline for a journalism course that was adopted throughout the city's high school system. Another fellow organized a weeklong workshop for teachers and student editors in an area of Northern California where little such work had been encouraged. Teachers in Illinois and New York prepared handbooks for editors of school papers. And some fellowship winners arranged student visits to newspaper plants.

The Newspaper Fund also sponsored two summer workshops in 1959, at what was then Texas A&M College and at

Syracuse University. Donald D. Burchard, head of the journalism department at A&M, called it a "stimulating project." Dr. Wesley C. Clark, dean of the School of Journalism at Syracuse, reported that the workshop there was "a worthwhile undertaking, and there is definite need for it in this area."

In addition, the Newspaper Fund provided one grant to support a study of journalism interest among high school editors attending a convention at Columbia University and another for the organization and operation of the Future Journalists of America, a new undertaking at the University of Oklahoma.

All these efforts, combined with the distribution of *Do You Belong in Journalism?*, greatly expanded awareness among the nation's editors and publishers of the Newspaper Fund's campaign to attract promising young people to journalism.

At its annual meeting in August 1959, the Association for Education in Journalism (now the Association for Education in Journalism and Mass Communication) commended the fellowship program. In a formal resolution, it hailed the program as "a significant step in upgrading instruction" in the high schools and predicted it would have "far reaching effects in recruiting for the profession."

This success spurred an expansion of fellowships, workshops and grants. For 1960, fellowships were to be offered to a minimum of 100 teachers. A seminar was organized at Indiana University, sponsored solely by the Newspaper Fund and tailored for advisers to high school newspapers.

That year, 316 teachers sponsored by the Newspaper Fund took summer courses at 41 colleges and universities. About 850 applied, nearly twice the number in the first year, and 340 were offered fellowships. The outlay was $160,000, an average of about $500 per teacher-fellow.

Kilgore was satisfied. "It has been most encouraging and stimulating to us to find so many who are doing such fine work in this field," he said. "I am sorry we couldn't do something for every teacher who is seriously interested in better training to teach journalism."

The Newspaper Fund approved grants for high school workshops again at Texas A&M and Syracuse and also the

University of Southern California and Chico State College in California. Matching funds were offered to the Ohio State University to employ a field secretary to work with high school journalism teachers and newspaper advisers. Financial support was also provided to the School of Journalism at the University of Oklahoma to help with the new Future Journalists of America organization.

J.L. O'Sullivan, dean of the College of Journalism at Marquette University, noted dramatic enrollment increases. He wrote to Carter: "I am sure you will be interested in our enrollment figures for this year. We have 45 male students out of a total of 113 in the freshman class. It is an increase of 15 men over last year. … I am confident that teachers who were at Marquette on *The Wall Street Journal* [sic] Fellowships helped a great deal in getting this large enrollment in freshmen."

In the program's second year, some colleges had already developed special summer offerings in journalism to appeal to Newspaper Fund teacher-fellows. At Nebraska, William E. Hall, director of the School of Journalism, reported an "all-out" effort to build on the early stirring of interest: "We're attempting to work through the administrator, the guidance counselor, the journalism teacher or publications adviser and the hometown editor."

Interest among parochial high schools was keen from the beginning. Among those in the inaugural class of teacher-fellows who took lessons back to school with them were Father Raymond of St. Bede Academy in Peru, Ill., who brought Karin Walsh, a Chicago journalist, to his school for a talk on journalism; Sister M. Laurentia of Scecina Memorial High School in Indianapolis, who worked with her school's guidance counselors to provide information and *Do You Belong in Journalism?* to students interested in journalism; and Brother Gerald Hagemann of Notre Dame High School in Biloxi, Miss., who shifted his school publication to letterpress printing.

Carter understood the importance of following through. During the fall of 1959, after the first summer of teacher fellowships, he started publishing and distributing a monthly *Newsletter* to each teacher. The purpose was to keep fellows in contact with one another and with the Newspaper Fund and to offer a clearinghouse for ideas about best practices.

In addition to informing the first fellows that they would be receiving complimentary copies of *Do You Belong in Journalism?*, an early *Newsletter* reported that Kilgore had received the Wells Memorial Key at the 50th anniversary convention of Sigma Delta Chi. It was the highest honor bestowed by the society. In presenting the key, awards committee chairman Mason Rossiter Smith praised Kilgore and the *Journal's* philanthropy:

> "The Newspaper Fund, another *Journal* venture, which among other things, encourages high school teachers to learn more of journalism through summer school scholarships at journalism schools, is another example of the efforts of a great newspaper and a great newspaperman…."

The *Newsletter* also informed the first fellows of possible repeat grants for teachers who devised outstanding programs for their students when they returned to school. The intent was to award only one grant of $1,000 for the most outstanding program. But at the conclusion of the 1959-60 school year, so many stimulating efforts had been undertaken that the Newspaper Fund board awarded special grants to 34 teachers. Carter judged that the most outstanding of these was William Nolan of Richmond, Calif.

JOURNALISM TEACHER OF THE YEAR

Nolan had been teaching at Harry Ells High School since 1951 but had never received formal training in journalism. He was planning a summer of driving a milk truck and taking journalism courses at the University of California at Berkeley when a student showed him an announcement from *The Wall Street Journal*.

It said high school journalism teachers could apply to the Newspaper Fund for grants to study journalism during the summer; Nolan was accepted. He used his $730 fellowship to take courses during the summer and fall semesters. "I thought taking these courses would enable me to answer questions from my students better," Nolan recalled more than 20 years later, by which time he had become *Dr.* Nolan and a school principal.

Most of the teachers who have benefited from Newspaper Fund fellowships, workshops, and literature during its first 50 years have fit a profile similar to Nolan's. He had no formal training in journalism but had worked at a local paper in Norman, Okla., as a high school student and while in college at the University of Oklahoma, where he studied geography and Spanish after World War II on the GI Bill.

At Ells, Nolan was teaching journalism to 35 students and advising the newspaper staff of *The Jolly Roger*. It wasn't until 1959 that, through the Newspaper Fund, he received any journalism education.

Nolan won recognition again in 1960, this time earning a $1,000 grant, for improving the school newspaper, bringing professional journalists into his classroom and helping several students choose newspaper careers. His visitors included local newspaper, radio and television journalists and a news writing professor from the Berkeley campus. "I had a broad spectrum of guests, and the students really enjoyed it a lot," Nolan said. "I had a half dozen students say it helped clarify their goals."

Thus was Nolan, an inaugural teacher-fellow, selected as the first National High School Journalism Teacher of the Year in an award program that continues today. The Newspaper Fund also selected teachers for smaller cash awards for meritorious achievement. In those days, the $1,000 teacher award prize went directly to the winner with no strings attached; a change in tax law for foundations eventually resulted in the money going to a teacher's school instead.

Nolan applied his award to fees and books at Berkeley while he pursued a master's degree and then a doctorate in secondary education. He loaded his program with journalism courses, and members of the journalism faculty served on his dissertation committee.

His doctoral study was about the preparation and experiences of high school journalism teachers in Northern California. He found his own experience to have been common. "Usually, if you ever had any acquaintance with a newspaper, you automatically became the journalism instructor at the high school," he recalled. Eventually, he set up the journalism department at Cabrillo Community College in Aptos, Calif. For many years, he *was* the journalism department, teaching two sections of newswriting and two in an introductory course while advising the student newspaper, *The Voice*. He retired in 1983.

BUILDING UP, REACHING OUT

The year 1959 provided a period of incubation and experimentation in which the Newspaper Fund tried to find ways of encouraging more talented young people to consider careers in journalism. The results were immediate and impressive. In a report, Carter described the Newspaper Fund's achievements for 1960, its first full year of developing some of the 1959 proposals.

The 1960 achievements included:

- Fellowships for 316 high school teachers taking summer courses in journalism at 41 colleges and universities. Twenty-nine of these teachers assembled at Indiana University in an experimental seminar.

- Specialized workshops for high school journalism teachers and school newspaper advisers. One workshop, at Iowa State University, accommodated 46 teachers and was fully underwritten by the Newspaper Fund. Others at the University of Southern California, Chico State College in California, Texas A & M, Syracuse University and Kent State University were partly supported through grants from the Newspaper Fund.

- Grants for advanced study awarded to the heads of two schools of journalism.

- Distribution of almost 10,000 copies of *Do You Belong in Journalism?*

- Providing a clearinghouse for journalism career information, including advice on where to get an education or a scholarship. Carter made himself available for talks to editors, publishers, educators, associations and organizations.

- Grants for experimental studies in journalism education: a "depth reporting" class project at the University of Nebraska, a high school journalism extension program in Ohio, a series of Saturday journalism classes for teachers in metropolitan New York and a proposal to develop school pages in local newspapers in Illinois.

The Newspaper Fund's approach under Carter became more comprehensive when it began in 1960 to reach out to higher education. The experiment at Nebraska represented a bold move into developing a journalism curriculum. The Newspaper Fund provided a $6,000 grant to develop an advanced course in news gathering and writing. The result was an in-depth reporting course that flourished through the 1967-68 school year. Students were instructed in writing more complex investigative or explanatory stories, and the money helped pay for field trips and travel as well.

Another outgrowth of the class was a textbook, aptly titled *Depth Reporting* and authored by Neal Copple, which was quickly adopted by more than 100 journalism programs. Copple, a veteran newsman-turned-educator, became the dean of Nebraska's College of Journalism. The Newspaper Fund invested $26,000 in the Nebraska project over the years, until Nebraska newspapers saw fit to begin supporting it themselves.

One student in that class in the early 1960s was James Risser. "I thought that the class was an inspiration, and it really, heavily influenced the way I worked later as a journalist," Risser told the Nebraska alumni newsletter. Risser had a long career as a public affairs and environmental reporter and Washington bureau chief for *The Des Moines Register*, winning two Pulitzer Prizes for national reporting, in 1976 and 1979, among many other awards.

REPORTING:
THE FIRST INTERN PROGRAM

In a crucial move under Carter, the Newspaper Fund decided in 1959 to begin promoting newspaper careers among young men at elite liberal arts institutions without journalism programs and where little recruiting had been done.

The Newspaper Fund was the first journalism foundation to promote summer internships in which college students with majors other than journalism could work on a newspaper. Participating news organizations would pay the interns their minimum wage; students who completed the internship satisfactorily earned a scholarship to be applied to the next year's cost of college. The program in reporting was the first of the college internship programs. The Newspaper Fund's paid, professional summer internships for college students in reporting and editing would come to constitute the core of the foundation's work over the next five decades.

The demand for young, talented journalists had far exceeded the supply coming out of journalism schools. Kilgore believed that elite liberal arts colleges and universities were the least likely to attract students interested in newspaper careers. Yet these students – all men, many attending Ivy League institutions – were considered the sort of "best and brightest" that newspaper executives desired.

"In the back of their heads, Barney and his editors thought that there was a lot of talent that attended colleges and universities which had no journalism school," Carter recalled. "And they particularly wanted the Newspaper Fund to appeal to those schools."

The reporting program was tailored for these students. Many were already active on their campus newspapers. But paid newspaper internships were virtually unheard of. The $500 scholarship that the Newspaper Fund was offering, along with the experience of actual newspaper work, could offset a student's need to find a paying summer job in an unrelated field.

A group of newspapers, sensing a chance to recruit college students from top schools, agreed to cooperate with the Newspaper Fund on an experimental basis.

The Newspaper Fund anticipated a maximum of 15 participants, but interest far exceeded expectations. Before entries closed, 130 students from 31 colleges had applied. The Newspaper Fund screened the applications and directed the outstanding students to the cooperating newspapers.

After filling these initial jobs, the Newspaper Fund found

jobs for many more qualified applicants. In some instances, the students, with the Newspaper Fund's approval, found their own jobs. In every case, the hiring newspaper selected its trainee and arranged salary and duties.

In all, 53 college students were placed with newspapers throughout the country for the Newspaper Fund's first reporting intern class in the summer of 1960.

Among the initial reporting interns was Richard J. Levine, president of the Dow Jones Newspaper Fund at its 50th anniversary in 2008 following a 40-year career as a correspondent for the *Journal* and senior news executive for Dow Jones. A sophomore at Cornell University in Ithaca, N.Y., with no formal college training in journalism but with substantial experience on the undergraduate campus newspaper, Levine obtained an internship at *The Ithaca Journal*, a small afternoon daily in the Gannett chain, as the telegraph editor and a sports reporter.

"I made up the front page, wrote headlines and reworked wire copy," Levine said. "I'd come in early and put the paper to bed." The idea, he wrote in his post-summer report in 1960, was "to throw myself into the heavy daily grind, to get away from the excitement of college journalism. The glamour is exaggerated, but the grind is fascinating."

"It was a wonderful experience," Levine said. "I made fast friends with some editors, and they increased my interest in journalism as a career. From that summer forward, I never had any doubt that's what I wanted to do. I was hooked."

Other early trainees that first year reported that they, too, were hooked. Joe Gillan of Ithaca College, who worked at the *Rochester Times-Union* that summer, wrote to the Newspaper Fund: "At the beginning of this summer, I thought I was interested in newspaper work. Now I know I am. I know this is what I would like to make my life's work."

Not all of the interns opted for the newspaper life. One of the trainees, Elliott R. Morss of Johns Hopkins University, spent the summer working at *The Patriot Ledger* in Quincy, Mass. He confessed to having "given little thought to making a career in journalism." He was compelled by his newspaper experience to consider applying for a journalism scholarship "after I complete one year of economics at Johns Hopkins." It may have been journalism's loss, but Morss had a distinguished career in economics.

Tim Conlon, a Wabash College student, found his place in journalism for a while. "It was the most worthwhile summer I ever spent," he wrote in his end-of-summer report. "This job confirmed my vocational desire in journalism, and as of right now, I plan to make my career in journalism – in news coverage and reporting."

After graduation, Conlon obtained his master's degree in communications theory and journalism from Stanford University. He served in the military and later became bureau chief for *Business Week* magazine in San Francisco. In 1985, he and a group of Kaiser Aluminum managers negotiated a leveraged buyout and created National Refractories & Minerals. He later started a management consulting firm.

Editors deemed the inaugural program a success as well. Typical was this assessment from James A. Woodworth, then editorial director of the Westchester County Newspapers in White Plains, N.Y.: "We are frank to say we could not be more pleased with the work of Stone (Ronald Stone, a Hamilton College student). If the Newspaper Fund succeeds in sponsoring and developing a succession of young Stones, it cannot help but provide a lift for the entire industry."

George D. Stuart, editor of *The Valley Daily News* in Tarentum, Pa., wrote to Carter: "This is the most promising newspaper recruit I have ever run across. He seems to have everything it takes…. We want to have him back each summer until he completes his college career. Then we'll be happy to welcome him to our staff as a regular."

And Vincent S. Jones, executive editor of Gannett Newspapers, pledged his company's continued participation with the Newspaper Fund, a partnership that would last for the next five decades: "The Gannett Newspapers will be happy to cooperate with your project to provide internships for promising students who attend colleges lacking journalism departments … you have hit on a fine device …."

The reaction was the same at Dow Jones. Reading the reports from trainees and their editors, Kilgore commented, "They are most encouraging." Funding would continue for another round in 1961.

The Newspaper Fund reporting program's class of 1961 included at least three young men who would go on to shape journalism at the national level.

Norman Pearlstine was a reporting intern for the *Allentown* (Pa.) *Call* and *Chronicle* while a student at Haverford College. He began his career as a *Wall Street Journal* reporter in Dallas, then Detroit and Los Angeles. He served as Tokyo bureau chief, managing editor of *The Asian Wall Street Journal*, national news editor in New York, editor and publisher of *The Wall Street Journal Europe* and managing editor of the *Journal* in New York. He also served as editor-in-chief of Time Inc. and as chief content officer of Bloomberg L.P.

Ervin S. Duggan was an award-winning editor of the campus newspaper at Davidson College when he became a reporting intern at *The Washington Post* in 1961. He was awarded a Newspaper Fund scholarship and used the money to study and travel in Europe. He served in the Army, then became a reporter for the *Post* from 1964 to 1965. He joined President Lyndon Johnson's staff, writing speeches and promoting legislation for the Great Society and the Corporation for Public Broadcasting. He worked for Sen. Adlai Stevenson in the 1970s, then served in the Carter administration. He was national editor of *Washingtonian* magazine from 1981 to 1986 and was a private media consultant when he was appointed to the Federal Communications Commission in 1989 for a five-year term. He then became president of the Public Broadcasting Service until 1999.

Loren Ghiglione traveled across the country as a junior from Haverford College near Philadelphia to be a reporting intern in California. "I went to college wanting to teach history, but the summer internship changed all that," Ghiglione said. "I worked for a California community newspaper, and it was great because the editor filled the paper with his humor, his feel for typography and his courage. I decided that someday I wanted to be like him."

After returning to Haverford to finish his senior year, Ghiglione began a career that included editing and publishing *The Southbridge* (Mass.) *Evening News* and owning its parent company, Worcester County Newspapers. He also presided over press associations, including the American Society of Newspaper Editors.

Ghiglione left newspaper management to begin a second career in journalism education. He directed the Annenberg School of Journalism at the University of Southern California for two years. He held the James M. Cox Chair in Journalism at Emory University in Atlanta and directed its journalism program for three years. In 2001, Ghiglione, who also held a J.D. from Yale University and a Ph.D. in American civilization from George Washington University, was appointed dean of the Medill School of Journalism at Northwestern University and served five years.

Ghiglione took a year's leave in 2006 to work on three books, then returned to teaching at Medill in the fall of 2007 as the inaugural Richard Schwarzlose Professor of Media Ethics. In the summer of 2007, he was named the first recipient of the Roy F. Aarons Award for his contribution to education and research on issues affecting gay, lesbian, bisexual and transgendered communities.

Recalling the start that the Newspaper Fund had given him, Ghiglione said: "Don Carter told me that if I could find a newspaper willing to employ me, he would give me a Newspaper Fund internship. Some 60 papers rejected me, but the *Claremont Courier* said yes. So Don – and Paul (Swensson) – kept their part of the bargain."

So did Ghiglione and so did the *Courier*, in the most generous way. At the end of his internship, Ghiglione signed over his $500 scholarship check to the newspaper and asked that the money be used to pay a Haverford man's intern salary there again. The Claremont newspaper honored Ghiglione's wishes. For the next two years, Haverford men spent their summer as Newspaper Fund reporting interns at the *Courier*: George F. Bagby Jr. in 1962 and Donald R. Moore in 1963.

The third class of Newspaper Fund reporting interns, in 1962, included many men who went on to success in journalism and other fields. First, though, they went to internships that summer in 30 states, Washington, D.C., Puerto Rico, and Israel. Josiah Lee Auspitz spent the summer at the *Jerusalem Post*. Since earning degrees, including a doctorate, from Harvard and Oxford, Auspitz has attained world renown as a philosopher and humanitarian.

But in this field of standouts in 1962, four later stood out particularly:

• **Joseph R. McGinniss** of the College of Holy Cross spent his summer at the *Port Chester Item* in New York. McGinniss, only a sophomore, had applied for a scholarship knowing that he was ineligible. But he pleaded his case eloquently in a letter to then executive director Paul Swensson to be considered anyway. On official stationery of the Holy Cross student newspaper, *The Crusader*, McGinniss wrote that he sought "actual experience" that would also solve "the sometimes knotty problem of summer employment" – both goals of the Newspaper Fund internship program. And he wanted this despite having "talked with quite a few men in the newspaper and magazine fields" who had been "to say the least … slightly discouraging. They harp upon the long, irregular hours and the low pay, and mention how hard it is to get ahead." McGinniss was accepted. After graduating in 1964, he went to work as a general assignment reporter at the Worcester *Telegram & Gazette* in Massachusetts. He left soon thereafter to become a sportswriter, as he had been for the bulk of his experience at *The Crusader*. After moving to *The Philadelphia Inquirer*, where he was a columnist, McGinniss, at 26 years old, wrote the blockbuster account of Richard Nixon's 1968 presidential campaign, *The Selling of the President*. He left journalism to write mainly nonfiction full time. His 1983 bestseller, *Fatal Vision*, an account of the Jeffrey McDonald murders, earned McGinniss further acclaim, but after he was sued by McDonald (the case was settled out of court), McGinniss became half the subject of Janet Malcolm's book, *The Journalist and the Murderer*.

• **David L. Shaw**, a student at Pepperdine College in California, spent his summer reporting for the *Los Angeles Mesa News-Advertiser*. He transferred to and graduated from UCLA. He also worked for the *Long Beach Independent* before joining the *Los Angeles Times*, where he distinguished himself as a media critic. He won a Pulitzer Prize in 1991 for his series examining coverage of the McMartin molestation case but earned greater industrywide praise for his 37,000-word analysis of the Staples Center advertising scandal at the *Times.* Although he was partly a pariah in his own newsroom, Shaw was a hero among most of his journalistic brethren. He was still a potent force for reform in journalism when he died in 2005 at 62 of complications from a brain tumor.

• **Nicholas Gage** of Boston University interned at the *Telegram & Gazette.* He later worked as an investigative reporter for *The New York Times* and specialized in Mafia affairs. But he won critical acclaim for two autobiographical memoirs, one of which was *Eleni,* an homage to his mother, who was executed during the civil war in Greece. The book was made into a film starring John Malkovich as Gage.

• **Michael Mukasey** was the editorials editor of the *Daily Spectator* at Columbia University before he interned with the United Press International wire service in Newark, N.J. After graduating the next year, Mukasey earned a law degree at Yale in 1967 and practiced in New York for 20 years before becoming a federal district court judge. In 2007, he became the 81st attorney general of the United States.

As for Carter, he had worked energetically to ensure that the Newspaper Fund's programs got off to a strong start. It provided grants to 875 high school and junior college teachers, and an additional 150 teachers attended publications workshops supported by the Newspaper Fund. In addition, 53 college students were sponsored for summer newspaper work in 1960, and 142 received scholarships in 1961. More than 100 newspapers worked with the Newspaper Fund in providing internships. Distribution of the vocational guidance book exceeded 10,000 copies.

Carter's hunger for the work in the newsroom led him to Kilgore's other new proposed venture at the time, *The National Observer.* William E. Giles, news editor in the *Journal's* Washington bureau, had been chosen as executive editor in July 1961 for the startup of the newsweekly, which came on Feb. 4, 1962. Giles wondered whether Carter was interested in the job of managing editor. Recalled Carter: "I asked him, 'When do we start?' He said, 'First you've got to find somebody to succeed you. And second, we do not want to make any announcement of this at all, until sometime far into the future. We want you to focus your attention now on finding a good successor.' "

The transition was immensely important. The Newspaper Fund position required a leader with Carter's enthusiasm for not only journalism but also recruitment and promotion.

Carter didn't have to think too long before coming up with the right name. "From my travels before and my association with newspapers, I knew Paul Swensson was a great choice," Carter said. "He was highly interested in education, even more than he was in working newspapers. He was a great teacher as well as a fine editor, but he preferred the teaching role."

Carter told the early fellows of the change in the October 1961 *Newsletter*. He described Swensson as "a fine newspaperman" and listed a full page of Swensson's achievements. About himself, Carter wrote only that he was "returning to *The Wall Street Journal* organization for a new executive assignment," a post that "involves the development of a new and significant publication that we believe will provide another step forward in American journalism."

After stepping down from the Newspaper Fund, Carter was elected to its board of directors, joining *Journal* editors, an honor that was extended also to Swensson and Tom Engleman when they resigned from the post.

After the *Observer*, Carter was editor of the *Bergen Evening Record* in New Jersey and *The Macon* (Ga.) *Telegraph* before becoming vice president/news for Knight-Ridder Newspapers in 1976.

After almost 50 years in journalism, Carter and his wife, Carolyn, retired in 1982 to their home on Sea Island, Ga. In 2004, they endowed the Carolyn McKenzie and Don E. Carter Professorship of Excellence in Journalism at the University of Georgia.

3

PAUL SWENSSON:
VISIONARY ARCHITECT

Barney Kilgore announced on Sept. 15, 1961, that Paul S. Swensson had resigned as managing editor of *The Minneapolis Star* to become executive director of the Newspaper Fund, succeeding Don Carter. Years later, then president Al Hunt would characterize Carter and Swensson as the Jefferson and the Madison of the Newspaper Fund. Swensson had joined the Minneapolis papers in 1935. He was managing editor of *The Minneapolis Tribune* from 1950 to 1955 and held the same position at the *Star* from 1956 to 1961.

He got his first taste of journalism at 15 as a correspondent for a Minnesota weekly. In 1928 he graduated cum laude from Gustavus Adolphus College, which later awarded him an honorary doctorate, and did graduate work at the University of Minnesota and the University of Stockholm. Now he was assuming leadership of a national foundation that sought to encourage students as young as 15 to begin considering newspaper careers.

Among Swensson's other qualifications were his connections in the newspaper industry. At the time of his appointment, he was a board memeber of the Associated Press Managing Editors and a member of the American Society of Newspaper Editors. He was immediate past president of the Minnesota professional chapter of Sigma Delta Chi and an active member on the national level.

Swensson inherited a program whose annual budget had grown to $250,000 from $80,000 in three years. (In addition to supporting the Newspaper Fund programs, Dow Jones & Co. provided office space at no cost and paid all of the administrative costs, including salaries, travel and entertainment.)

The future looked bright and challenging. Soon after starting work at 44 Broad St., however, Swensson lost Pat Kennedy, who had been Don Carter's able assistant, to a call-up by the Air Force Reserves. By late December 1961, however, Swensson told the Newspaper Fund's board of directors that another young man from Penn State had received clearance from his draft board to come aboard Jan. 2, 1962, temporarily replacing Kennedy, until August.

That young man was Edward Trayes. Although his stint lasted less than a year, Trayes would return to the Newspaper Fund several times in the 1960s and would eventually establish the first editing intern program at Temple University in 1968. Swensson was grateful to have Trayes's help.

Trayes's tenure with the Newspaper Fund has been nearly as long as Carter's. Trayes's first assignment, from January to June 1962, left a lasting impression on him. "I had such a privilege, to work with Paul Swensson," Trayes recalled fondly. "He was my very own professor. And just a really good man."

After that initial contact, Trayes said, "There wasn't a time when I wasn't in touch or consultation with Paul Swensson." Their meeting might never have happened had Trayes not one day walked past the office of John Vario, a Penn State professor. "He lifted his head and looked up at me, just at the exact moment I was walking past his open door," Trayes recalled. "He said that he had received notice of a position at the Newspaper Fund that sounded just right for me."

Swensson was on the road constantly, cultivating the seedbed for training and education. In 1962, he traveled 79,000 miles and spoke to audiences totaling 30,000 at 132 meetings. He appeared before statewide high school student organizations and addressed professional societies that shared his passion for bringing talent into journalism. He visited 51 college campuses where Newspaper Fund Fellows were studying.

The first statistical evidence that "this experiment might be working," Swensson said, came in a September 1962 survey by the Newspaper Fund to determine the number of college freshmen who were enrolling as journalism majors. Forty colleges and universities where journalism was being taught reported enrollments in the fall of 1962 were higher than the year before; 24 said enrollment had stayed the same, and eight reported declines.

A major issue in those years was the Newspaper Fund's focus on liberal arts students. Journalism deans began urging the Newspaper Fund to accept their students as well.

In 1964, the Newspaper Fund was helping 108 young men from *non*-journalism schools find summer jobs that year. Despite the Newspaper Fund's emphasis, a survey it made in April that year counted 795 news internships for *journalism* students. This was not a competition but a complement; a study had found that journalism graduates in 1964 filled only one of every seven available newspaper reporting jobs.

The role of women in the early years of the Newspaper Fund is both controversial and obscure. In 1962, for example, more than 50 women applied for an internship but none were selected. A 1963 memo, however, indicated that women were not formally excluded. In advance of a Newspaper Fund board meeting, Swensson wrote to Buren McCormack, vice president and editorial director of *The Wall Street Journal*:

"The permission of the Board to extend 1963 summer intern scholarships to a few young women has been exercised in two cases. The young women are:

"**Sondra Gail Wilson**, Wilmington College (N.C.) who will work this summer for the *Star-News* Newspapers at Wilmington, N.C.

"**Ann Fleisher**, Barnard College, who will work for the Moreau Publications at Orange, N.J.

"Both are women of unusual ability; arrangement for their summer jobs has been worked out with the respective executive editors."

No documentation exists to suggest that this special permission was exercised. Neither the women's names nor the names of their newspapers or schools appear in the official annual report for that year.

While the Newspaper Fund wasn't helping young women, it was helping another underrepresented group – blacks.

Swensson was especially proud of the role he played in helping Carl Rowan, who had been a copywriter, into the position of staff writer at *The Minneapolis Tribune* in 1950. Rowan, a pioneer African-American journalist, became a high-level appointee in the Kennedy and Johnson administrations.

Their relationship, in turn, influenced Swensson in the 1960s when he began thinking about how to encourage minority students to consider journalism and how to create opportunities for them. Swensson had also been affected by the liberal politics of fellow Minnesotans Hubert Humphrey and Orville Freeman.

One of Swensson's visionary ventures was the sponsorship of the first summer workshop at Savannah State College for Negroes in Georgia in 1964.

A visit to Georgia the previous year had impressed on him the need to help teachers and students at the nation's historically black colleges. "Here was a large body of bright people who could really contribute to the profession, but no one had invited them," Swensson said years later.

During his visit, Swensson spoke to 1,200 students, faculty members and others who filled the auditorium at Savannah State for a high school press day. His talk was broadcast by radio to an estimated 12,000 listeners.

He gave his popular "The Face of a Newsman" speech, in which he described the nose for news, the discerning eye, and the chin for courage. According to Swensson, it was the first effort to encourage black high school students to consider news careers beyond black newspapers. The Savannah State faculty and the high school teachers, Swensson said, "were fascinated that anybody wanted them." And so did Swensson begin to build the Newspaper Fund's relationship with Savannah State in particular and with black colleges in general.

He recalled the repugnance of segregation. He could neither

sit in the front seat of a car driven by a black journalism teacher nor in the back seat with the teacher's wife. Because he was lodged in the city's top hotel, his hosts could not visit him in his suite or be served in the coffee shop.

After returning from his first trip to Savannah, Swensson asked Bill Clabby, assistant managing editor of *The Wall Street Journal's* Southwest edition, to speak to black students at Bishop College in Dallas.

"I really didn't know what to talk about," Clabby recalled almost 20 years later. "I didn't think the students would believe me when I told them we wanted them in our profession. This was 1963. Dallas was heavily segregated. You couldn't even take black guests into clubs. Why should the Bishop students think we wanted them in our newsrooms?"

More than a hundred students and teachers came to hear about careers in journalism. By evening's end, Clabby was convinced that the Bishop students were interested in the Newspaper Fund's programs. Swensson considered the Bishop event the kind of breakthrough he needed to move the Newspaper Fund toward a different kind of recruiting.

Among the 19 teacher workshops Swensson proposed and carried out for the summer of 1964 was a trial program at Savannah State for African-American teachers and some of their students in southeastern states.

One of the participants was a Savannah high school student, Wanda Smalls, who later attended Spelman College, became a Newspaper Fund editing intern in 1970, and – 40 years after that first Savannah workshop – was appointed managing editor of the *Montgomery* (Ala.) *Advertiser*, after a distinguished career at *USA Today*.

For each of the next five years, more than 20 teachers and students, black and white, enrolled in the workshops, producing a lab newspaper titled *The Journalist*.

The Savannah State seminars marked the start of the Newspaper Fund's formal minority-recruitment program. Swensson envisioned what would eventually become the Urban Journalism Workshops as a concept similar to the teacher workshops. "Teachers in the urban centers have to be tremendously dedicated to work in that environment," Swensson said in an interview with the magazine *C:Jet*. "It needs to be said over and over, 'The Newspaper Fund believes in you and is willing to put money into making you a better teacher.'"

In late 1967, *Newsweek* reported that Ed Cony, *The Wall Street Journal's* managing editor, had made a special plea that fall: "We would like to step up our efforts to attract Negro reporters. If anyone has any ideas as to how we might do a better job in locating prospective Negro applicants, we'd be much obliged to hear about them." *The Journal*, *Newsweek* pointed out, had immediately identified four candidates, thanks mostly to recommendations from the paper's younger staffers.

The Washington Post, *The New York Times*, and *The Newark News* had been actively recruiting black reporters for some time, according to *Newsweek*. The Midwest's largest newspapers "suddenly" discovered Lincoln University in Jefferson City, Mo., which had an enrollment of 2,000 students, about half of them black.

By 1967, Swensson had begun planning the first Urban Journalism Workshop at American University for the summer of 1968. He knew about the groundbreaking research being conducted by his protégé, Ed Trayes of Temple University. As early as 1968, Trayes had begun surveying journalism majors and tracking the responses of black students among them. His findings were bleak: Just 2% of students planning newspaper careers were black.

The workshop at American University was conducted before the ink was dry on the historic Kerner Commission report by the National Advisory Committee on Civil Disorders. President Johnson had created the commission on July 28, 1967, in the wake of summer riots in the black sections of many major cities, including Los Angeles, Chicago, Detroit and Newark. Better known today as the Kerner Report, taking its name from the commission chairman, Illinois Gov. Otto Kerner, the report was issued on Feb. 29, 1968. It concluded that urban violence reflected the profound frustration of inner-city blacks and that racism was deeply embedded in American society.

The Kerner Commission found that newspapers were

"shockingly backward" in seeking out, hiring and promoting blacks and other minorities. The report further suggested that the high school was the place to begin to solve the problem.

The program Swensson devised seized upon that recommendation. Inspired by Kathleen Zellmer, a Washington, D.C., high school teacher who had attended a Newspaper Fund workshop at American University in 1965, the first Urban Journalism Workshop was placed there. The Washington newspapers supported it. The Newspaper Fund's board did, too, urging Swensson to encourage black youth to consider journalism careers.

Twenty black students and one white student attended the first such workshop. They covered the Poor People's March on Washington and City Council meetings. They covered fashion, music and the workshop itself. The result was an aptly named workshop laboratory newspaper, *The New Voice*.

Swensson did not expect a quick fix or panacea. "We have to wait six to eight years to see if we've produced results," he said.

Yet the Newspaper Fund's minority-oriented programs began to produce results almost immediately. One example involved Zellmer and her student Ernest Tollerson. At the 1965 workshop, Zellmer had received instruction that helped improve her writing and editing. She returned to high school better prepared to teach her students those skills as they produced the school paper. Zellmer's work as a journalism teacher earned her honors from the Newspaper Fund for the next three years. Along the way, she encouraged Tollerson to study journalism.

The summer between his junior and senior years in high school, Tollerson attended the first Urban Journalism Workshop in 1968 at American. He said that workshop, along with his experience on the school paper and Zellmer's initial encouragement, sparked his interest in newspaper work. In 1973, Tollerson was named a Newspaper Fund reporting intern while attending Princeton University.

He went on to attend Columbia University's Graduate School of Journalism. He began his career in journalism in 1975 at *The Wall Street Journal*, then worked at *The Home News* of New Jersey and *The Philadelphia Inquirer* as a political reporter. He became editorial-page editor at *New York Newsday* and later served two years as a member of the editorial board of *The New York Times* before leaving for policy-and-research jobs and, eventually, a public affairs directorship with the Metropolitan Transportation Authority in New York City.

For the reporting intern program in 1967, the Newspaper Fund prepared mini-biographies of the young men who were chosen. The bio written about Marc William Salganik, a junior psychology major at Brown University, typified the credentials of a promising Ivy League student. One of Salganik's English professors wrote: "An extremely competent writer, both in the classroom and in the features and news columns of university paper. A hard worker. Baltimore native was high school newspaper editor; is editor of university daily. Seeks work in Northeast, but will work anywhere." Bill Salganik distinguished himself during a long career at Baltimore's *Sun*, with stints as an editorial writer and business reporter before retiring in March 2008.

A good deal of interest in journalism persisted at the Ivies and other liberal arts schools through the 1960s. To fan that interest, the Newspaper Fund continued offering $500 reporting intern scholarships to young men who were juniors and usually editors at their campus newspaper.

Application forms became available each fall through college placement offices and college newspapers. Deans of schools not on the mailing list began beseeching the Newspaper Fund to let their students participate. The best of the applicants were selected in January. By February, each candidate received a list of newspaper editors who had promised friendly consideration of a job application. But it was up to the student to nail down the job. At the end of the summer, the student was required to report to the Newspaper Fund on his internship. It then sent a $500 scholarship check to the student.

The Newspaper Fund's intern prize competition, initiated in 1965, was open to any college student, regardless of sex or academic major. These students did not need to apply to the Newspaper Fund for forms or help finding a summer position. The conditions instead included finding their own job writing or editing news. Midway through the summer, the student's managing editor could nominate him – or her – for a prize. The nomination, which was due by the end of July, required a letter from the supervisor and a 750-word essay by the nominee. Winners of 15 prizes of $500 each and 10 of $250 were announced by Sept. 1.

Eventually, there were 10 $500 prize winners, 15 $250 winners and 10 $100 winners. The outlays increased by 50% to almost $10,000, and it proved to be money well spent. Among prize winners in 1967 were:

• **James Benton** of the University of North Carolina, who became a director at Common Cause in 2002 after a distinguished career as a reporter;

• **Jerome "Jerry" Ceppos** of the University of Maryland, who rose to vice president/news at Knight-Ridder and in December 2007 became journalism dean at the University of Nevada-Reno;

• **Robert Hooker** of Davidson College, who became a top editor during a long career at the *St. Petersburg Times*;

• **Jack Fuller**, a Pulitzer Prize-winning editorial writer and editor and publisher of the *Chicago Tribune*; and **Judy Kulstad**, now Judy VanSlyke Turk, director of Virginia Commonwealth University's School of Mass Communications. The two were contemporaries at Northwestern University.

THAT CHAMPIONSHIP SEASON

Major changes in the Newspaper Fund's leadership took place in 1968. Barney Kilgore had died from cancer in late 1967, and Bill Kerby, his successor as chairman of Dow Jones, now also presided over the Newspaper Fund's board. Paul Swensson resigned in September 1968 after seven years as executive director and was succeeded by his young assistant, Tom Engleman, as the Newspaper Fund entered its second decade.

There were also major changes in the offerings with the launch of the Urban Journalism Workshops and the editing internship program.

The Newspaper Fund sponsored the intern prize competition for students for the last time in 1968 but again with remarkable results. Among the top prize winners were James Crutchfield of Duquesne University, an intern at the *Pittsburgh Press*, and Mario Garcia of the University of South Florida, an intern at the *Miami News*.

Crutchfield started his career as a reporter for the *Pittsburgh Press*. He spent the next three decades mostly as an editor at newspapers in Detroit; Akron, Ohio; Long Beach, Calif.; and Philadelphia and wound up back in Akron, becoming publisher in 2001. He joined the Cronkite School in the spring of 2007 as a visiting professor in journalism ethics and director of student media.

Garcia was nominated by the *Miami News*, where he had interned for consecutive summers. Managing Editor Howard Kleinberg was effusive about Garcia's work and work ethic, his maturity and bilingualism as a Cuban exile, and his ability to lay out and edit the business section without supervision. When it came to projecting what Garcia might someday become, Kleinberg wrote, "I think Garcia has a definite future in the newspaper industry." That future began after graduation with his first job at the *News*. Forty years later Garcia was the most accomplished newspaper designer in the world, with eight books and more than 450 redesigns to his credit and stints on the faculties of Syracuse University and the Poynter Institute.

In its four years, the intern prize competition recognized 130 students for their internship performance and provided $40,000 in prizes. The money for this program was shifted to the expanded reporting and editing programs for 1969.

EDITING:
START OF SOMETHING BIG

Even as he was pioneering in recruiting and training minority journalism students and teachers in the turbulent late 1960s, Swensson in 1968 began a unique copy editing internship program for all college students to fill slots that were going begging on America's copy desks, which were seen as less glamorous than reporting positions.

It seemed a radical experiment to place inexperienced college students alongside veteran editors, long considered guardians of a paper's credibility. The Newspaper Fund's board of directors was supportive. "The lack of interest in editing careers is something that concerns us greatly," board President Kerby wrote at the time. Swensson persuaded newspapers editors to agree to try it. "The practice up to that point was that that was not the way to do it," Swensson recalled more than 20 years later. "But the shortage was so great, and we were able to find so many bright young minds that the program did get kicked off."

Trayes, by then teaching at Temple University, recalled that Swensson was pleased with the success of the Newspaper Fund's reporting program but had felt something was needed for the other side of the newsroom desk. "It was an exciting concept, but lots of people said, 'I'm not so sure,'" Trayes said.

The Newspaper Fund editing internship program turned 40 years old in 2008, testimony to the success of Swensson's experiment.

To get started, Swensson asked Trayes if he could set up a residential workshop, or residency, at Temple that would offer newspaper editing interns top-flight training before going on to their summer work.

Trayes created the program and worked with Prof. Gene Gilmore of Illinois in 1968. Prof. Jack Botts set up a parallel program at the University of Nebraska, where Neal Copple, who in the early 1960s had taught a depth reporting class underwritten by the Newspaper Fund, was dean.

Those first on-campus residencies were three-week seminars. Thirty editing interns were chosen from among 101 nominees from 71 campuses. In striking contrast to the demographics of the reporting program, 12 of the editing interns – 40% – were women.

In addition to requiring a faculty recommendation for applicants, Swensson and his assistant Tom Engleman used questionnaires to measure the intensity of the students' interest in newspaper editing careers. They examined scholastic performance, explored students' reading habits and asked them to list their strengths and weaknesses as campus journalists, as students and as individuals.

"Those were real dynamo learning experiences," Swensson said. "The young people that came into them caught on to the idea that they were in an experimental program and that if it worked, it was going to be important to them."

Trayes remembered the interns working with wire machines clacking away in a glassed-in room. "We kept them busy day and night," he recalled.

At Temple, 14 students, 11 of whom were journalism majors, arrived June 7, 1968, for the first training residency. The three non-majors came from colleges with no journalism courses but had experience working on their college newspapers. Instruction at the residencies included editing basics, along with work in headline writing, libel, newspaper organization, typography and makeup.

There was a daily critique of *The New York Times* and *The Philadelphia Inquirer*, each of which was delivered to the classroom. Interns were challenged to "play editor," to consider news play and story content. Students and their instructors debated journalism ethics, the pressures on the press, and trends in newspapers. The group considered what newspapers might be like in 10 or 20 years, when, if journalism took hold in their lives, they might be among the managers in newsrooms.

Some students chafed under the repeated drills of editing error-filled stories, contending that no desk would receive such bad copy. Two students, in anonymous critiques, complained that the work was too hard. The only legitimate gripe was that they had arrived for training not knowing where they were headed at the end of the three-week residency. Assignments were determined after Trayes and Gilmore had had a chance to assess each intern and match them with newspapers.

The Temple interns that year were dismissed a day early, Friday, June 21, so that they could begin travel the next day to their newspaper assignments and be ready to begin work on Monday, June 24. They went off to, among other publications, the *Rochester Democrat & Chronicle; Rochester Times-Union, Binghamton* (N.Y.), *Press, Hartford Courant, Providence Bulletin, The Record* of Hackensack, N.J., *Suffolk Sun; The Wall Street Journal; Newark News; Philadelphia Bulletin; Baltimore Evening Sun; Washington Star; Richmond Times-Dispatch;* and *The Charlotte Observer.*

A few days after they started work, Gilmore began meeting with each intern and, wherever possible, the managing editor, news editor, or slot editor who had some chance to observe the interns' work. In every case, the interns had been greeted warmly, Gilmore found, "even the girls who were invading previously all-male territory."

Engleman proclaimed in the fall of 1968 the one-year "experiment" a success. In his report, Engleman assessed and summarized the inaugural editing program, incorporating feedback from editors, interns and the editing professors.

The interns followed the summer schedule suggested by the Newspaper Fund and found the time spent with different editors and desks to their liking:

> Copy editor: 2 weeks
> Makeup editor: 1 week
> Teen editor: 1 week
> Features desk: 2 weeks
> Picture desk: 2 weeks
> Sports desk: 2 weeks
> City desk: 2 weeks

In general, the editors were pleased with the interns and the training they received. Some editors suggested that the training be shortened so that the summer work could be longer.

The interns described the seminars as "very useful tools of instruction" and the work rewarding. Some sought more lab work and practical exercises; others thought too much of the course was spent on editing and suggested a broader introduction to the news world. The first two classes of editing interns included:

• **Jennie Buckner**, who trained at Temple and interned at *The Charlotte Observer* and rose to become editor of the paper and vice president/news of its parent company, Knight-Ridder. In 2006, she served a semester as Davidson University's Batten Professor of Public Policy.

• **Marty Claus**, who trained at Nebraska and interned at *The Wichita Eagle*, rose to vice president/news for Knight-Ridder, a position she held from 1993 to 2000. After graduation from Michigan State, she was a writer and editor for the *San Bernardino* (Calif.) *Sun-Telegram*, a Gannett newspaper, from 1970 to 1977. She joined the *Detroit Free Press* in 1977 and held editing positions there until 1987, when she was appointed managing editor for business and features. Claus was among the first 10 journalists inducted into the Features Hall of Fame in 1997 by the American Association of Sunday and Feature Editors.

"People now in hiring positions at newspapers were in this program," Trayes recalled years later. "You can go into any newsroom and find people who have gone through this program."

The 30 editing interns in that inaugural year of 1968 came from 29 different institutions. Only the University of Missouri produced two interns. "I know of no School of Journalism which pays more attention to editing than the University of Missouri," Swensson wrote. "It did not surprise me a few weeks ago when two Missouri Journalism students received internships in the Newspaper Fund's first experimental editing program." In 2007, a record 17 Missouri students became Newspaper Fund editing interns, out of a total 107 nationwide.

Missouri gave the Newspaper Fund an award during the school's Journalism Week in 1968 for its efforts. It cited the Newspaper Fund's "imaginative yet practical efforts in devoting nearly $2.5 million to encourage talented young people to select journalism as a career; its successes in upgrading high school journalism programs by providing summer grants for journalism study to nearly 5,000 teachers and publication advisers since 1959"; and "its internship program, which has enabled 678 college students to work a vacation period on daily newspapers."

It wasn't until October 1968 that the Newspaper Fund announced that journalism majors would be considered for the reporting intern program for the first time the next year. Thirty-three women were among the 1969 participants. They included Karen Elliott and Pamela Hollie, who would use their Newspaper Fund internships as springboards – Elliott to a *Wall Street Journal* career as a Pulitzer Prize-winning reporter, editor and publisher, and Hollie as a business writer and editor for both the *Journal* and *The New York Times* and director of several prestigious foundations.

One of the 1968 reporting interns was William G. Keller of Pomona College, who interned at the *Oregonian* in Portland. After stints at *Congressional Quarterly* and the *Dallas Times-Herald,* Keller spent two decades as a Pulitzer Prize-winning reporter, editor and columnist for *The New York Times* before ascending to executive editor in 2003.

STEPPING DOWN, NOT OUT

While he was preparing to resign as executive director, Swensson prepared a modest report for Newspaper Fund President Kerby in June 1968 that included a list of project proposals that might be carried out:

1) Preparation of reports
2) The *Newsletter*
3) Teacher workshop proposals
4) Junior college institute proposals
5) The 10th anniversary commemoration
6) Teacher of the Year award
7) Teacher achievement certificates
8) Teacher conventions to be attended
9) Journalism school conventions to be attended
10) Professional conventions to be attended
11) Intern scholarship program
12) Intern prize competition
13) Editing internships
14) College writing awards
15) Career literature
16) Career film program
17) Newsroom clinics
18) Summer travel in 1969
19) Negro recruiting

The 19th, Swensson wrote, was an "added starter."

4

TOM ENGLEMAN:
MASTER BUILDER

Thomas E. Engleman was named executive director of the Newspaper Fund in 1969, succeeding Paul Swensson.

His accomplishments in that position built on the plans of Don Carter and Swensson. During the Engleman era, the Urban Journalism Workshops grew from the experimental first program at American University in 1968 to as many as 32 in a single year. The editing intern program expanded, and programs for minority college students were initiated. Engleman also successfully demonstrated that high school journalists were good students – they fared well in competition to become Presidential Scholars and scored higher than others on college entrance exams.

Engleman earned his bachelor's degree in English from Emory and Henry College in Virginia, where he was a student of George Crutchfield's. Crutchfield had met Swensson at the annual Sigma Delta Chi convention in Minneapolis in 1967 and learned that Swensson was looking for a new assistant to replace Pat

Kennedy, who had been tapped by Dow Jones & Co. to become the company's director of communications. Crutchfield suggested to Swensson that Engleman, who was a copy editor at *The State* in Columbia, S.C., would make a good assistant.

Engleman was reluctant to leave South Carolina but agreed to an interview with Swensson. The announcement of his hiring was made on Dec. 21, 1967. Engleman was still working on a master's degree in journalism from the University of South Carolina, and he would finish his thesis while working for Swensson.

Engleman's first Newspaper Fund assignment was to read the bundles of high school newspapers that arrived from around the country. He was to select the articles and photos he found most interesting and to forward them to Swensson for a publication called *These Struck Our Fancy*, a feature that continues to appear as part of *Adviser Update*, the Newspaper Fund's quarterly publication. Engleman also wrote for *Newsletter*, the monthly publication mailed to high school teachers who participated in the Newspaper Fund's summer workshops and seminars. Carter had started the tradition in 1959 after the inaugural program as a "newsletter" to the first group of teacher-fellows. Now, the mailing was in the tens of thousands.

Swensson sent Engleman on his first field trip to the editing intern residency at Temple University. Engleman's copy editing stint at *The State* had lasted two and a half years before he was called to the Newspaper Fund. "So watching how Gene Gilmore and Ed Trayes co-taught newspaper editing was a wonderful experience," Engleman recalled.

Engleman also went to American University in Washington, D.C., that summer to visit the first Urban Journalism Workshop for high school students. The program held a special interest for Engleman, whose thesis was about the racial integration of South Carolina's newspapers and broadcast stations. Swensson asked Engleman to help him select the 1968 National High School Journalism Teacher of the Year. In the fall, Swensson included Engleman again in the selection of reporting and editing interns for the next summer's programs.

When Swensson announced in the summer of 1968 that he was leaving the Newspaper Fund to teach journalism at Temple, he recommended to the board of directors that Engleman be appointed acting director to succeed him in the fall.

Engleman was not an obvious choice to succeed Swensson. He lacked the years of newsroom experience, the national reputation and the network of contacts of Swensson and Carter. Engleman seemed positively boyish, but he didn't lack support. "You will find Tommy vigorous and enthusiastic," Swensson wrote to President Bill Kerby. "He will not disappoint you."

A year later, on July 18, 1969, Kerby announced Engleman's promotion to be the Newspaper Fund's third executive director.

In Engleman's early years the editing intern program grew rapidly. Temple became the center for the East, and Nebraska the Midwest. Residencies at Ohio State University and the University of Nevada-Reno were added to cover the "mid-East" and West, respectively.

The training courses were trimmed to two weeks from three for financial reasons and to ensure that interns were left with at least a 10-week window for summer work afterward. Since only college juniors were eligible at the time, they would be expected back on campus for the fall semester. Also, the practice of waiting to assess students and match them to their newspapers during the final week of training was ended in favor of assigning them when they were first chosen.

Reports from newspapers were glowing. By the mid-1970s, about 90% of the editing program's alumni had been offered and accepted editing jobs upon graduation. The program was proving valuable also because few college journalism departments at the time were teaching editing. Swensson and Jack Botts had experimented with an advanced editing course at Nebraska, but it had not caught on the way the depth reporting course there had a decade earlier, so funding for it was discontinued.

The University of Nevada-Reno residency was added in 1969, and the number of interns nationwide grew to 44. It was directed by Larue Gilleland and Ted Conover.

One of the Nevada-Reno residency's interns that first year was Howard Finberg, who spent the summer at *The Oregonian* while a student at San Francisco State College. Finberg, now a newspaper futurist, has spent almost 40 years exploring ways to improve journalism. "And it all started with an editing pencil," Finberg said in an interview. "From the beginning, I loved the language, loved working with words." His passion earned Finberg a start on the features desk of *The Oregonian*. He spent much of the next three decades in senior newsroom positions at *The Arizona Republic*, the *San Francisco Chronicle*, and the *Chicago Tribune*. Finberg also left his mark at the *San Jose Mercury News*, *San Francisco Examiner* and *The New York Times*.

At every step, he was at the forefront of advances in technology. Recognized in 2000 with a New Media Pioneer Award, Finberg was appointed Presidential Scholar at the Poynter Institute in 2002. In 2008, he was directing Poynter's e-learning project, NewsU. Finberg had come full circle since his Newspaper Fund days.

Three special programs received Newspaper Fund grants in 1970: the Blair Summer School for Journalism, a program for outstanding students held at Blair Academy in Blairstown, N.J.; the Sacramento State College Depth Reporting Project; and an experimental student newspaper co-sponsored by *Newsday*.

The annual program at Blair was supported by grants from newspapers that sponsored students from their particular cities or areas. The six-week program provided instruction and unique opportunities to meet and talk with the country's top journalists.

The depth reporting project gave upperclass students a chance to experiment with journalistic writing techniques. To reach high school students on Long Island, N.Y., the Newspaper Fund co-sponsored with *Newsday* a training program for seven students who gathered news for an experimental newspaper published five times during summer 1970. The idea was to teach high school students about the newspaper publishing process.

That same year marked a "million" milestone for the Newspaper Fund's career film *Did You Hear What I Said?* Through Dec. 31, more than 1.3 million people had seen the movie, which was filmed on location and without a script. It followed a beginning *Nashville Tennessean* reporter on his first big assignment. The film was broadcast on television 167 times in 1970. It was one of 22 titles from a library of career "literature" published or distributed by the

Newspaper Fund in 1970. In all, more than a quarter-million pieces of career information were distributed that year.

The Newspaper Fund experimented with a unique advertising venture in 1971. It invited advertising students in college journalism programs in the spring to submit advertisements designed to encourage young people to consider newspaper work as a career. The Newspaper Fund judged the 94 entries received from 16 schools and chose five to send to newspapers and trade publications that had consented to use them as "house ads," or free filler for unused space in their news columns. The five winners each received a scholarship.

By 1971, the editing intern program had become the Newspaper Fund's major undertaking and expense. Running a residency was costly. In just its third year, the program had doubled in size to 60 interns, surpassing the 54 in the reporting program. The Newspaper Fund held the line on spending in 1970 despite adding a fourth editing internship residency. Interns continued to be paid a living wage, with salaries averaging $126 per week.

An editing residency was awarded to Dr. John Clarke at Ohio State. Clarke, an 18-year newsroom veteran at newspapers such as the *Providence Journal-Bulletin* and *The Scranton* (Pa.) *Times*, joined the faculty at Ohio State just three years before the Newspaper Fund came calling. Clarke had "more professional experience than 95% of the people teaching," Trayes said.

That experience included sharing a Pulitzer Prize for deadline reporting when he was working in Providence in 1953. Clarke was covering police and city hall when he reported from a house where a bank robber was holed up. The writer was Ben Bagdikian, who went on to work at *The Washington Post* and served as dean of the University of California Berkeley's Graduate School of Journalism. "I was the guy who just happened to be there," Clarke recalled.

Among his first students at Ohio State was William Tillinghast, a graduate teaching assistant when Clarke advised the *Lantern*, the campus newspaper. Tillinghast, who became a director of a Newspaper Fund editing residency at San Jose State University in 1985, recalled a time when *Lantern* staffers created picture pages using Shakespearean references.

Clarke, a literary scholar with more than a passing knowledge of the Bard, critiqued the work and corrected their errors, much to his students' surprise. "One of my interests has been the literary and aesthetic dimensions of journalism," said Clarke, who pursued a doctorate in American and English literature at Brown University while working nights at the Providence paper.

Even after moving on to the University of Scranton, Clarke continued to direct the program at Ohio State, retiring after 22 years and seeing his 1991 interns off to their summer jobs.

Ken Kilbert was a 1976 editing intern at *The Roanoke Times* who trained under Clarke and turned to a career in law. Kilbert recalled that compared with his journalism classes at Bethany College, the two-week training at Ohio State was "so much more intense, and the other interns were so bright and skilled, that I had to learn a lot fast or be left in the dust."

Kilbert said he was reminded of Clarke "pretty much every time I watched *Lou Grant*. He was great. Gruff on the outside and soft on the inside, with a ton of experience and insight, usually conveyed via a humorous story." The other interns also appreciated Clarke. "I recall all of us pitching in to buy him a large bottle of Chivas Regal at the end of the session," Kilbert said.

A year after his Newspaper Fund summer, Kilbert began his journalism career as a reporter at the Zanesville, Ohio, *Times Recorder*, covering cops and courts. "My Newspaper Fund experience was a keystone of my journalistic training," he said. The courthouse beat, though, had piqued his interest in the law. As much as he enjoyed "the newspaper gig," Kilbert resigned to go to the University of Pittsburgh School of Law, where his journalistic training served him well when he edited the law review.

"I have often said that my journalism training was a great advantage to me" in a law career, Kilbert said. "Among other things, you learn to be inquisitive and discerning, to ask the right questions of the right people so that you have complete and reliable information. I often would use 'who/what/when/where/why' as a guiding principle when doing depositions or interviews, to separate wheat from chaff quickly, to write in a logical, organized fashion – don't bury the lead! – that is clear, crisp and powerful, and to edit accordingly."

Despite leaving journalism for law, "editing remains in my blood," Kilbert said. He edited a Pennsylvania Bar Association newsletter, *Civil Litigation Update*, for four years and in 2007 was co-editor of the American Bar Association's *Environmental Litigation Committee Newsletter.*

For two generations, Clarke trained Newspaper Fund editing interns and molded future leaders. Among them:

• **Laura Landro**, a 1975 intern for the *Pittsburgh Press* who became senior editor in charge of entertainment, media and marketing coverage in a career of more than two decades at *The Wall Street Journal.*

• **Melissa McCoy**, who interned at *The Columbus Dispatch* in 1986 and went to work at the Long Beach *Press-Telegram*, where she was a copy chief and news editor, before moving on in 1992 to the *Los Angeles Times* as a copy editor on the metro desk. Within two years, she was the foreign desk copy chief; and in 2001 she was appointed assistant managing editor of the copy desks, which was then a rare title in newsrooms. By 2005, she had become deputy managing editor.

Students nationwide were finding a stint on the copy desk rewarding. "A copy desk on a good newspaper is no graveyard, as many students think," said Mark Eicher, a Michigan State student who trained at Nebraska and interned at the *Detroit Free Press* in 1970. "Copy editing is an art, and it can be fun."

Said Lucinda Jonsson, a University of Southern California student who trained at Nevada-Reno and interned at *The Salt Lake Tribune*: "I had harbored the suspicion that copy editing might be dull, but I got a very pleasant surprise. It was tremendous."

In 1973, a residency proposal came from George Crutchfield at Virginia Commonwealth University. While teaching at the University of South Carolina, Crutchfield had recommended Engleman to the Newspaper Fund. In advance of the 1973 board meeting, Swensson cautioned that a Crutchfield proposal would be considered "automatically suspect" and "favoritism" by "more than a few casual friends in and out of journalism education."

Swensson had a second concern about the VCU proposal: "a tie-up, directly or indirectly, with the Richmond newspapers." Crutchfield proposed visiting these Media General newspapers and using them as a site for interns. Swensson mentioned what he called the newspapers' "undistinguished day-to-day performances in editing, makeup and layout," though he praised their editorial pages.

In the end, the board approved the VCU proposal. And the surviving newspaper in Richmond remained a Newspaper Fund participant through its 50th anniversary year.

Other problems, sometimes tempests in teapots, arose over the years. For example, in a Feb. 18, 1977, letter to then Newspaper Fund President Ed Cony, Swensson noted a long-simmering resentment between editors at a major newspaper chain and the Newspaper Fund, though the paper had continued to take editing interns. Issues included editors nitpicking interns' performance; limiting access to the residency director when he visited during summer; the Newspaper Fund's method of recruitment; and an objection to the $500 scholarship for the Newspaper Fund's intern while the paper's other interns received nothing. Swensson replied that the Newspaper Fund would not object if the paper gave its other interns similar scholarships.

One feature of the editing program in its first 25 years was the on-site visit that the residency directors paid to the interns at their newspapers. The visits allowed the residency directors to see first-hand how the interns were adjusting, whether they were given challenging work and whether they were performing to the best of their ability.

The directors also used the visits to learn about each newspaper's editing operation to ensure that the interns' preparation was appropriate. Directors also could meet with newspaper executives to encourage continuing support of the program.

Clarke, for example, would arrive at the paper in the afternoon to meet executives, some desk editors and the intern and would sit in with the intern if invited. When visiting interns working nights at morning papers, Clarke would return after dinner with the intern and a supervisor to meet senior editors who might only then be coming on for a shift.

Although extremely rare today, afternoon or evening papers were common among the program's participants in the 1970s. Visits to them sometimes meant arriving at the newsroom shortly after dawn to get a full picture of the intern's duties and performance. Because of the fast pace of the work, introductions and meetings often came after the last deadline, when lunch or dinner could be arranged.

All internships in the college programs required a written end-of-summer report by the intern and an evaluation by a newsroom supervisor. A one-page evaluation of one editing intern in the 1970s began, "Again the Fund has lived up to its reputation of sending the best interns .... [The intern] has performed admirably and ranks right up there with the previous two interns and in some ways surpasses them. His editing techniques are sharp, he has a fine command of the language and spelling and grammar. His layout is strong, if not flashy."

Another from the same era: "Her work was certainly acceptable, but not brilliant. Her superiors found her reluctant to challenge copy, reluctant to seek their advice. Because of her shyness, perhaps she gave the impression of not being very interested in the internship." The former intern mentioned above had a stellar career in journalism and, later, teaching. The latter transcended her shyness to become a star journalist at a major newspaper and, later, at one of the world's largest online news organizations.

MINORITY PROGRAMS: A MAJOR PRIORITY

The Newspaper Fund worked throughout the 1970s with local newspapers to expand its Urban Journalism Workshops, sponsoring 12 workshops for 214 high school sophomores and juniors in 1970. One of them, Franklin Smith of Plant City, Fla., said of his two-week session at the University of South Florida in Tampa: "Considering the fact this was my first real involvement with journalism, questions that I didn't know were answered, and things that weren't clear are now coming clear to me. I really feel that I learned a lot, and I have seriously thought about continuing work in journalism."

The number of workshops had grown from one pilot effort in 1968 to four programs in 1969 to 12 in 1970. The number of students served that year was more than twice the 99 participants of the first two years.

A survey from the first two years showed that all but one of 40 respondents planned to go to college, and 22 said they planned to major or minor in journalism, with 16 saying they wanted to work on campus newspapers. In 1972, 10 workshops accommodated 217 high school students, most of them black or from other minority groups. That year, a follow-up survey of the now more than 300 participants from 1968 to 1970 showed that 58% planned to study journalism in college, with 63% hoping to work on campus newspapers.

Following the Kerner Commission's report, other programs for minority journalists and journalism students emerged quickly, if only briefly. Foundations besides the Newspaper Fund began making grants to universities to support education and recruiting efforts. For example, a Ford Foundation grant financed a program at Columbia University for black students interested in broadcasting careers. Columbia's journalism enrollment was 15% black in 1970.

In a speech that year in Princeton, Swensson had noted that less than 2% of American news staffers were black. Among daily newspapers with a circulation of more than 10,000, only five had blacks in executive roles. A snapshot of the nation's journalism schools wasn't any brighter: Fewer than 250 blacks were enrolled, less than 1% of all journalism students. A few pockets of hope existed at Columbia and at New York University in the East and at Michigan and Illinois in the Midwest. The University of Texas-Austin and Baylor University were providing assistance for Spanish-speaking and black teachers and students.

In the South, the picture was much bleaker. The Newspaper Fund's workshops at Savannah State were reaching dozens of teachers and hundreds of students. But the state's largest newspapers, the *Atlanta Journal* and *Constitution*, had yet to change. During the Ralph McGill-Eugene Patterson era, the newspapers were widely acclaimed for their support of the civil-rights movement, and individual journalists there had volunteered time to teach at student conferences. But management hadn't funded minority journalism education programs.

The University of Georgia journalism school had graduated the distinguished Charlayne Hunter (now Hunter-Gault), whose matriculation in 1961 had ended segregation at the institution. It was beginning a campaign to attract bright black students. The University of South Carolina was moving even faster, operating a federally financed program to provide journalism training for black high school teachers.

The Newspaper Fund reported that a decline in minority hiring in the 1970s paralleled a reduction in the number of programs and scholarships for minority journalism students. In 1972, spending for such special programs was estimated at $255,000; by 1977, that figure had fallen to about $115,000. The American Society of Newspaper Editors Committee on Minorities urged in 1978 that the "commitment to recruit, train, and hire minorities ... urgently ... be rekindled." It called such a move "simply the right thing to do" as well as "in the newspaper industry's economic self-interest."

The Urban Journalism Workshops were shortened to two weeks from three to allow for more within the same budget. Logic suggested that more, if shorter, workshops, would benefit more students. Engleman argued that the Newspaper Fund would need to continue to sponsor them since most newspapers weren't providing grants.

In an Oct. 10, 1973, letter to Dow Jones President Warren Phillips, Engleman noted that the *Journal* had hired only two black Newspaper Fund interns in five years. Engleman alerted Phillips that at the November board meeting, he would propose to continue the workshops, expand a visitation program and invite Newspaper Fund alumna Pamela Hollie to become a board member.

The board approved all three requests.

In 1973, the Newspaper Fund had experimented with a program involving minority high school students during the school year. The High School Visitation Program brought young minority journalists into selected Los Angeles and Philadelphia high schools to work with students and advisers and to plan, produce, and critique their school newspapers. The professionals' visits were paid for by the Newspaper Fund, and local newspapers were asked to provide free time for the reporters, who received honoraria.

Research on newspapers' minority hiring prepared in 1977 by ASNE showed about 2.5% of the nation's 38,000 newsroom professionals were non-white – a tiny portion, but more than double the 1% of the early 1970s. In their first 10 years, the Newspaper Fund's minority initiatives had accommodated more than 1,300 high school students. More than 100 of them were working in or preparing for journalism careers.

By 1978, the Newspaper Fund also was working with the National Association of Black Journalists, which was founded on Dec. 12, 1975, to build a network of journalism workshops staffed by minority professionals. They provided instruction and counseled students interested in journalism careers.

PASSAGES

In the same time period, newspapers' interest in the Newspaper Fund's reporting program, its first college journalism project, had begun to wane. With the number and quality of college journalism students increasing, many newspapers were at last finding it easier to recruit talent on their own. "Newspapers could choose between hiring a journalism student committed to working in journalism and hiring a liberal arts student who was just testing the waters," Engleman said in an interview. "The choice was easy."

The teacher workshops and seminars also declined in the 1970s. More colleges and universities were offering summer workshops for local journalism teachers. The number of applications to the Newspaper Fund fell, and by the end of the decade the board of directors decided to devote more resources to the editing program and the Urban Journalism Workshops.

The experimental series of "institutes" for community college journalism teachers ran for four years but was discontinued because of cost. Still, those community college institutes, first operated at the University of Texas by Jack Dvorak, led to the creation of the Community College Journalism Association, which continues today.

THE TEMPLE OF EDITING

The editing program held steady through its first decade, with the number of slots ranging from 39 to 60.

Trayes's program remained a model. For four decades, top newspaper editing professionals visited Temple to help train Newspaper Fund interns: William G. Connolly, retired senior editor of *The New York Times,* and Merrill Perlman, chief of copy desks at the *Times.*

Trayes and his guests worked the interns from 8:30 a.m. to 5:30 or 6 p.m. each day, including weekends. Still, he found time to introduce them to the fun side of Philadelphia: a tour of the Liberty Bell, a taste of a cheesesteak hoagie "if they did OK."

In 1990, Trayes took the interns to Gannett Co. headquarters in Rosslyn, Va. The group toured *USA Today* and Gannett News Service, lunched in the executive dining room and met with editor Peter Prichard and editors from other Gannett newspapers.

Former Newspaper Fund intern Kathy Kozdemba, an executive in Gannett's news division, coordinated the visit. She invited the interns as a "way to show them internships are important in terms of career development and to show that there were people who have moved up through the ranks." They also met former Newspaper Fund interns Emilie Davis, then managing editor/operations at Gannett News Service; Barbranda Lumpkins, special projects editor for *USA Today's* Life section; and Dorothy Bland, managing editor of the paper's library services.

One of Trayes's early interns was Jerry Schwartz, who attended the 1976 residency. He interned at the Associated Press in New York and returned to the wire service after graduation. He has been a writer and editor there for three decades. He has also taught feature writing at New York University and has assisted Trayes at Temple. He is the author of the *Associated Press Reporting Handbook*, widely used in journalism classes.

THE RESIDENCY EXPERIENCE

The 1979 editing residency directed at Virginia Commonwealth University in Richmond by Bill Turpin and

Don Carter (above) and Paul Swensson (right) were the first two Newspaper Fund executive directors. Al Hunt, a past president, referred to Carter and Swensson as "the Jefferson and the Madison" of the Newspaper Fund.

The Founders of the Fund.
Top: Robert Bottorff and William
Kerby; (center): Bernard Kilgore;
(bottom): Buren McCormack
and Vermont Royster. Kilgore,
the chairman and chief executive
of Dow Jones, called a lunch
meeting in December 1958 at
which the broad outline of the
Newspaper Fund was drawn up.
The group formalized the plan at a
meeting on Jan. 28, 1959, and the
Newspaper Fund was born.

Bonnie Datt gets some pointers from fellow intern Christopher Myers at the 1993 St. Bonaventure University editing training center.

Jill Wheeler, a senior at South Dakota State University, was one of 56 students who participated in the Newspaper Fund's 1985 editing intern program. She spent the summer at the *Deseret News* in Salt Lake City.

Students from the 1986 Hugh N. Boyd Urban Journalism Workshop at Rider University visit *The Philadelphia Daily News* to interview editors and reporters.

Jackie Engel, the 1979 National High School Journalism Teacher of the Year from McPherson (Kan.) High School, discusses a story with a student editor.

Ron Kitagawa, a student at the University of California at Santa Cruz, spent the summer of 1990 as an editing intern at the *Press-Telegram* in Long Beach.

High school journalism teachers brush up on their skills at a 1975 workshop at California State University, Fullerton.

Prof. George Crutchfield, who directed editing workshops at Virginia Commonwealth University and Florida Southern University, discusses the program with a potential intern.

Patricia S. Graff, the 1995 National High School Journalism Teacher of the Year, addresses her peers in Kansas City at the Journalism Education Association national convention.

Participants at the Oklahoma State University Workshop for Teachers pose in front of the School of Journalism and Broadcasting. Director Mike Sowell is standing at the right in the front row.

Directors of the 2006 editing intern programs met shortly before Christmas to select more than 100 students. Front row: Leslie Guevarra, *San Francisco Chronicle;* Diana Stover, San Jose State University; Bill Tillinghast, San Jose State University; Griff Singer, University of Texas; and Brian Brooks, University of Missouri. Second row: Rich Holden; Charlyne Berens, University of Nebraska; Rick Kenney, University of Central Florida; Joe Grimm, *Detroit Free Press*; Bill Cloud, University of North Carolina; and Ed Trayes, Temple University.

Newspaper Fund Deputy Director Linda Shockley (left) and Executive Director Rich Holden (second from right) get together with several high school teachers of the year—Don Bott, 2002; Steve O'Donoghue, 1990; Terry Nelson, 2001, and Robin Sawyer, 2000.

Newspaper Fund Deputy Director Linda Shockley (foreground) poses with Jan Maressa, who served as the office manager of the Newspaper Fund for more than 30 years. Maressa was in Phoenix to celebrate Shockley's receiving the 2000 Robert Knight award from the Association for Education in Journalism and Mass Communication.

Robin Sawyer, the Newspaper Fund's 2000 High School Journalism Teacher of the Year from Manteo (N.C.) High School, exchanges greetings with President George W. Bush at the annual conference of the American Society of Newspaper Editors.

Executive Director Paul Swensson (front row center with folder) traveled thousands of miles to meet with participants in the high school journalism teacher program during the summer of 1962.

The Newspaper Fund board members gathered for a group photo prior to the 1994 annual meeting.
In the front row are, from left: Al Hunt, Rich Holden, Everett Groseclose and Tom Sullivan; second row; Sharon Murphy, Linda Shockley and Barbara Martinez; third row; Larry O'Donnell, Don Carter, Paul Swensson, Don Miller, Peter Kann and Robert Bartley.

Diane Hall of Florida A & M University listens as Joe Blake of *The Philadelphia Daily News* talks about issues he faces in his high school journalism workshop. Sharing in the discussion at a 1993 conference are Larry O'Donnell, a past president of the Newspaper Fund, and Robert Woods of the University of Missouri.

Dr. John Clarke shows Allison Inserro how to operate a video display terminal during the 1988 editing intern training program at Ohio State University.

Linda Cooksey of Jonesboro (Ark.) High School gets some help from lab assistant Ray Hopfer at a Desktop Publishing Workshop at Southern Oregon University in 1999.

George Taylor, the 1985 National High School Journalism Teacher of the Year, and his wife, Mary Ruth, accept the award from Tom Engleman, executive director of the Newspaper Fund, and Uzal Martz (right), publisher of the *Pottsville* (Pa.) *Republican*. Today, Taylor is the editor of *Adviser Update*, a quarterly Newspaper Fund publication for high school journalism teachers and advisers.

Dr. Rick Kenney, left, a professor at Hampton University and the author of *"COPY!"*, meets with Kenn Altine, a Newspaper Fund alumni and director of editorial development for Hearst Newspapers.

Homer Hall of Kirkwood (Mo.) High School jumps for joy after he was named the 1982 National High School Journalism Teacher of the Year.

Ed Trayes, a Temple University professor who has directed intern training programs for more than 40 years, prepares to select next year's crop of students.

Professors from 12 historically black colleges and universities gathered in July 2009 for a multimedia training seminar ar Western Kentucky University

High school journalists nationwide worked to provide coverage of the tragedy on Sept. 11, 2001. *The Spectator* is a student publication of Stuyvesant High School, which is near the World Trade Center site.

administered by Crutchfield provides a picture of a typical editing program.

Crutchfield, whose demeanor, appearance, and speech have always suggested that he had been sent from central casting to play a Virginia squire, drilled interns constantly on style, spelling and general knowledge. He found teachable moments in common conversations and would politely but firmly correct the misuse of, say, "different than."

Crutchfield was also a master of organization and detail. He oversaw the residency and helped with intern selection. He reviewed applicants' exams and scoured their resumes. And he critiqued their essays for commitment to an editing career.

"That's what the program was about" he said. "I tried to screen out students who really wanted to be reporters but sought the cachet that comes with having a Newspaper Fund internship on one's resume. And the essay had to be sterling, mistake-free, really, to earn consideration."

At colleges across the country, prospective interns were studying for the exam and completing applications and essays. The application was scored for a student's academic and practical experience. Students who had been interns or who were the publisher, chairman, or editor-in-chief of their campus paper or had worked more than 40 hours on their paper earned five points for each of those achievements. Completed coursework in journalism skills meant three additional points, as did declaring a journalism major and having experience with a video display terminal.

The applicants' 500-word essay required a statement addressing one of four points: their most satisfying experience in journalism; why they wanted and needed the internship; their philosophy toward newspaper editing and reporting; or how the internship would help them achieve their career goals.

Performance on the editing test, which Engleman introduced in 1977, was crucial. Errors in spelling, redundancy, libel, irrelevancy and news judgment were embedded in a story double-spaced on one side of a sheet of paper. Applicants were expected to correct these mistakes.

Finally, two letters of recommendation from professional editors or journalism professors were required.

VCU trained 10 of the 40 editing interns in May 1979. They came from colleges as large as Alabama and Kentucky and Maryland and as small as Bethany College in West Virginia.

Crutchfield had been hospitalized for open-heart surgery the day before the residency began. That left Turpin not only to direct the program and provide most of the instruction, but also to run VCU's journalism program until Crutchfield returned. Turpin benefited from the invaluable assistance of Greg Brock and Dan Shorter, two alumni of the Newspaper Fund's internship program. They returned annually to Richmond with the support of their newspapers in Charlotte and West Palm Beach, respectively.

Brock was an intern at *The Palm Beach Post* in 1974 as a student from the University of Mississippi. He worked at *The Washington Post, The Charlotte Observer,* and the *San Francisco Examiner* and was awarded a Nieman Fellowship at Harvard in 1994-95. He joined *The New York Times* in 1995 and was deputy political editor, then news editor in its Washington bureau before he was appointed a senior editor in May 2006, helping to oversee the *Times's* standards and ethics.

Shorter was a former student at VCU who had attended the training residency at Missouri in 1977. Shorter interned at *The Palm Beach Post*, returned to a full-time desk job there after graduating, and made a career as an innovator in emerging newsroom technologies for Cox Newspapers. He rose to become general manager of PalmBeachPost.com, which has won more than 25 awards. From 1978 to 2002, Shorter returned to the Southern region residency each May. "I've hired dozens of Fund interns," he said in 1995.

Brock and Shorter checked the interns into new residence halls for married and graduate students at VCU, then led them to Turpin's house for a cookout that evening. The interns met Turpin, who until then had been a gruff voice on the phone, and his wife, Bonnie.

Interns were warned to be prepared for a "crash course" in editing. Could they explain the distinctions among "feel," "think," and "believe"? What was Harry Truman's middle name? Could they help prevent a libel suit?

Just as important was the interns' preparation for editing local copy. What did they know about their newspaper's stylebook and the newsmakers in those towns and cities? What about place names? Each intern was expected to show up with a "funny facts" notebook of information most relevant in their newspaper. When Engleman visited, he would quiz the interns on geography and the spelling of place names. Woe to the intern who didn't know whether the town in Florida was spelled Juno Beach or Juneau Beach!

Training began at 8 each morning, with a four-hour editing session before lunch. Afternoons were more informal, featuring professional journalists from Virginia newspapers. On a day trip to Fredericksburg, Va., and Washington, D.C., the interns met publisher Charles Rowe and managing editor Bob Baker of the *Free Lance-Star* and sat in on a late-afternoon news meeting at *The Washington Post*.

There, one starstruck intern was intrigued by a bulletin-board memo signed by Bob Woodward. Another wanted to stroll over to the Style desk to catch a glimpse of Sally Quinn. The evening was capped with dinner at Blackie's House of Beef in Washington before the return to Richmond.

One 1979 VCU intern, Tony Fargo from Morehead State University in Kentucky, spent the summer on the copy desk of *The Tampa Tribune*. He later worked as a newspaper reporter in Florida and eventually became a scholar of media law. In 2008, now *Dr.* Fargo was on the faculty of Indiana University's journalism school.

"I can clearly remember the terror during boot camp of having to write an accurate, good headline in what seemed like a minute," recalled Anne Glover, who interned at the *Norfolk Ledger Star* in 1981. "And then Bill Turpin would give us instant, and quite often brutal, feedback. It could not have been a better gift. I have retained that ability to let the words wash over me, absorbing whatever lesson they hold."

After graduation from Ole Miss in 1982, Glover joined the *St. Petersburg Times*. She became one of the first women promoted to newsroom management at the *Times* and held the title of assistant managing editor/copy desks. She was a founding editor of **tbt*, the *Times's* alternative free weekly-turned-daily and in 2008 was assistant managing editor/online features at tampabay.com, the paper's online site. Glover is grateful for the Newspaper Fund's network of journalists. "I am never far from a friendly face or a resource I can reach out to," she said.

Carole Tarrant, a West Virginia University undergraduate, studied under Turpin and Shorter and Edmund Arnold at the VCU residency and interned at *The Newport* (Va.) *Daily News.* "It made me a better writer and gave me a broad view of the paper from my first year as a professional," Tarrant later recalled. "Shorter ran the show. I remember it being tough – enough with the impossible headline counts! – but I still carry the lessons with me today."

After graduating from West Virginia, Tarrant went to work as a copy editor and page designer at the *Montgomery* (Ala.) *Advertiser.* She then went to *The Tampa Tribune*, where she spent more than 13 years in a variety of positions, including copy editor, reporter, bureau chief and team leader, before becoming managing editor of *The Forum* in Fargo, N.D. In 2005 she became managing editor of *The Roanoke* (Va.) *Times.* Known for her innovations in digital publishing, she was promoted to editor in early 2007 and led the newspaper's widely acclaimed coverage of the Virginia Tech shootings.

Crutchfield, now retired and living with his wife, Francine, near Virginia's James River, recalled fondly the annual December reunions in Princeton with the other residency directors. Once the business dinner was completed, they could be found caroling around a brightly lit Christmas tree in Princeton. Over time, in the interest of decorum, probity and age, and tempered by more moderate budgets and beverages, the annual selection meetings became more subdued.

A LITERATURE REVIEW

Literature financed or published by the Newspaper Fund grew into the nation's primary source of information about journalism careers. The annual survey of journalism school students provided data about placement of graduates. The Newspaper Fund also helped the Association for Education in Journalism and Mass Communication to publish its annual report on journalism school enrollments. *The Journalism Scholarship Guide,* once a thin, pocket-sized publication, expanded with the increase in the number of journalism programs and their enrollments. The name eventually changed to *The Journalist's Road to Success: a Career Guide* and included articles about how to write a resume, what courses to take in college, and the benefits of an internship. Single copies of the guide remain free.

REPORTING: THE END OF AN ERA

The reporting program ended in 1978. Interest in reporting internships was still keen, but enough newspapers were recruiting their own reporting interns and running their own programs. The final two years of the reporting program were as strong as ever, with positive results.

In 1977, the roster included three who would go on to success at Baltimore's *Sun* papers: Mark Hyman, Pat Meisol, and Derek Reveron.

Among the 18 interns in the program's final year in 1978 were Caesar Andrews of Grambling State University and *The Wall Street Journal* and Dorothy Bland of Arkansas State University and the *Memphis Commercial Appeal*. Both became publishers in the Gannett newspaper chain. Another was Ruth Marcus of Yale University and the *Journal's* Washington bureau. She became an editorial writer and columnist at *The Washington Post*.

5

ENGLEMAN:
THE SECOND DECADE

In 1978, the Newspaper Fund's board approved a minority editing program to begin in 1979 at the University of Kansas for students who were enrolled in graduate studies or who planned to do so.

In that first class was Deborah Heard, who interned at the *Saint Paul Pioneer Press*. "I discovered I loved the copy desk," Heard told the Newspaper Fund. She received her master's degree from the University of Missouri. She was a copy editor and then night city editor at *The Miami Herald*. Hired by *The Washington Post*, she rose to deputy assistant managing editor for Style before taking a buyout in 2008.

Patricia Marroquin was in the 1980 program, interning at *The Wall Street Journal*. She landed on the copy desk of the *San Jose Mercury News*. "Without the Fund's program, I wouldn't have been able to get a job at the *Mercury*," Marroquin said three years later. She was a founding member of the American Copy Editors

Society and worked at the *Los Angeles Times* before becoming the business news copy chief at *The Dallas Morning News*.

Malrey Head, who had just graduated from Spelman College in Atlanta, wasn't convinced that newspaper work was in her future until her editing internship. "At one time, I thought I was in the wrong field," she said. "But I am now convinced after this summer that journalism is what I want to do." After graduate studies at the University of Missouri she became an editor at the *Atlanta Journal and Constitution* and then moved to cnn.com.

After three years at Kansas, the program moved to New York University, where it was directed by Prof. Joshua Mills, later assisted by Prof. Mary Quigley. The program was a success. After five years, more than 70% of its alumni had gone on to full-time jobs in newsrooms.

The Urban Journalism Workshops were equally successful. In 1985, a record 145 newspapers teamed with the Newspaper Fund to co-sponsor 24 workshops attended by 384 students.

By that year, Engleman calculated that the Newspaper Fund was directing nearly 40% of its annual outlays toward minority projects. "The bottom line," he said, is "how many young people are touched through our programs and publications. If that is the way we measure success, the Dow Jones Newspaper Fund will come out on top of everybody's list."

Also in 1985, the board of directors of the National Association of Hispanic Journalists decided to contact the several groups operating programs for minorities to urge that Hispanics be considered for board positions. Engleman received a call from Guillermo Martinez of *The Miami Herald*. Engleman told Martinez that the Newspaper Fund considered minority groups in all of its programming decisions. For example, of the 16 minority students chosen for the 1985 editing program, six were Hispanic, five were African-American and five were Asian-American. The Newspaper Fund was, once again, ahead of the curve on minority issues.

In the early 1990s, Knight-Ridder Inc. gave the Newspaper Fund a $50,000 grant to support high school workshops in or near cities where Knight-Ridder owned newspapers. That enabled the Newspaper Fund to support seven new workshops. In all that year, the Newspaper Fund awarded almost $115,000 to 32 workshops serving more than 600 students. A few years later, Knight-Ridder committed $85,000 over three years, and the John S. and James L. Knight Foundation added $50,000.

The Urban Journalism Workshops are deeply rooted in their communities.

In Philadelphia, the program, held in the newsroom of *The Philadelphia Daily News*, celebrated its 20th anniversary in 2006. Mister Mann Frisby attended the workshop when he was a high school student, graduated from Penn State and began his career at the *Daily News* in 1997. He immediately began mentoring students in the same program he had attended. He left the paper in 2000 to become a novelist and in late 2005 published *Holla Back...but Listen First: A Life Guide for Young Black Men*.

The Philadelphia project was founded by Don Williamson, who developed a proposal for the workshop during the city's newspaper strike in 1986. Williamson had worked at the University of Kansas Urban Journalism Workshop. He started a program in San Diego when he left Kansas for the *San Diego Union* in 1984, so it was logical for him to start a program in Philadelphia when he arrived there.

The Marquette University Urban Journalism Workshop also celebrated its 20th anniversary in 2006. Twenty-nine alumni returned to the Milwaukee campus and heard the keynote speaker, Stanley Miller, a 1994 alumnus and deputy business editor at the *Journal-Sentinel*, proclaim: "Journalists, at their heart, are teachers. They just use a different medium. So the opportunity to engage young people in a venue like the journalism workshop is a real treat for all of us."

A minority reporting intern program for college sophomores was instituted in 1986, eight years after the original college program for reporting interns had ended. The program was patterned after the minority editing program that had been running successfully since 1979. The internship training was directed by Prof. Harry Amana at the University of North Carolina. Amana had moved to Carolina in 1979 from Temple University, where he worked with Trayes.

Among the eight students chosen for the minority reporting

internship program that first year was Darryl Ewing of the University of Texas. He spent the summer at the *Atlanta Journal and Constitution*, where he loved the job and his editors loved him. "Working at a major newspaper this summer has moved me closer toward a career in journalism," Ewing wrote in his end-of-summer report to the Newspaper Fund. "The experience at the *Journal and Constitution* will help me in applying for future internships and employment."

Ewing's assignment editor, Susan Soper, told the Newspaper Fund that he came to the job prepared to jump into the routine of reporting and writing. "He always approached his assignments seriously and professionally." He was commended for his story on tampering with over-the-counter medicines.

In 1987, Ewing applied for an editing internship and was assigned to *The Des Moines Register*. He trained at Missouri.

"The thing I remember most about the workshops was realizing how much I really didn't know," Ewing recalled 20 years later. "And the workshops inspired me to work harder on filling the knowledge gaps in punctuation, grammar and style once I got back to school. The other thing that sticks with me about the program was the opportunity to work with major news organizations in other parts of the country. For me, that experience was invaluable and made a large world seem much smaller, particularly through the eyes of a college student who had not traveled much outside of Texas. I still maintain contact with my roommate in Iowa when I was an intern at *The Des Moines Register*."

The reporting residency program was shifted in 1989 to Missouri, where it was run by Prof. Gail Baker Woods. The minority reporting program eventually was modified to a scholarship-only competition, which allowed more students to benefit. Grants of $1,000 each were awarded to students who obtained internships and applied successfully to the Newspaper Fund for support. By 1990, the program was benefiting 20 students.

One was Jemele Hill, a Michigan State undergraduate who spent a summer at *The Lima* (Ohio) *News*. "I didn't have a lot of money," Hill recalled. "I grew up on welfare and was raised by a single mother. Winning that scholarship was huge from that perspective. It also encouraged me to keep going. I had heard all the horror stories about what journalists make out of college, so you feel a little anxious about what you're getting yourself into. Dow Jones gave me the confidence to continue to pursue my dream."

For Hill, that pursuit began as a general assignment reporter for the Raleigh, N.C., *News & Observer*. Later, she covered Michigan State football and basketball for the *Detroit Free Press* before moving to the *Orlando Sentinel* in 2005, where she wrote a sports column. Less than two years later, at just 30, Hill went to espn.com and *ESPN the Magazine*.

While at the *Orlando Sentinel*, Hill worked with an editor who had, in sports terminology and his own words, "hit for the Triple Crown" with the Newspaper Fund.

Lynn Hoppes was an alumnus of an Urban Journalism Workshop at Western Kentucky University in 1984, a reporting intern at *Newsday* in 1987 and an editing intern at *The Washington Post* in 1988. "When I was in high school, I wasn't an avid journalist," Hoppes recalled. "But I got involved in the Urban Journalism Workshop program because my teacher forced me. Well, I stunk. I got one scholarship to go to college … $400. That was it."

Still, Hoppes was admitted to Western Kentucky University, where he was encouraged to apply for a Newspaper Fund minority reporting internship. He was selected to spend the summer of 1987 at *Newsday*. Hoppes recalled his odyssey this way: "Drive up to North Carolina for training. Meet an eventual girlfriend. Drive to New York to work for *Newsday*. Yep, *drive* to New York. Brought everything in my car. At *Newsday*, my car breaks down." But, he added, "I enjoyed myself."

Later that year, Hoppes earned a Newspaper Fund editing internship for the summer of 1988. He recalled that when the Virginia Commonwealth editing residency director told him he would be interning at *The Washington Post*, Hoppes replied, "Is that in Seattle?"

After graduation, he worked as a copy editor at *The Courier-Journal* in Louisville, then joined the *Orlando Sentinel*, where he rose through the ranks of the sports department. In 2007, he was named associate managing editor of sports after serving as executive sports editor for eight years. "Now I'm sports editor of the *Orlando Sentinel*, and my staff has won more than 100 awards," Hoppes said, his self-effacing nature giving way to pride in the work of those around him. "So, it was a good foundation."

Some high school students who attended Urban Journalism Workshops found fame elsewhere.

Erika Harold, who attended an Urban Journalism Workshop at Eastern Illinois University in Charleston in 1996, was chosen as Miss America in 2003. As a junior at Urbana High School, she wrote in her application that the program would be "an ideal experience" that "would enable me to make a well-informed decision about the path I choose to take in my future."

Her ambition, she disclosed, was to become a lawyer, and studying journalism first would help her "learn such skills as gathering information and synthesizing it into a logical, coherent article." Harold graduated Phi Beta Kappa from the University of Illinois and, after delaying her enrollment to serve as Miss America, she attended Harvard Law School.

Another successful Newspaper Fund alumni was Reggie Rivers, who attended a high school workshop at San Antonio College in 1985 and, as a senior that year, wrote obits for the *San Antonio Light*. Before graduating with a journalism degree from Southwest Texas State University six years later, he interned with the *Austin American-Statesman* and *Newsday*. "The Urban Journalism Workshop I attended in 1985 was one of the most productive journalism exercises I have ever been involved in," Rivers told the Newspaper Fund the year he graduated. "I really learned a lot there, and I was fortunate to be able to build on that foundation with further experience at metropolitan newspapers."

Two decades later, Rivers was still putting his training to good use as a weekend sports anchor for CBS4 in Denver after a five-year career in the National Football League. Aware of his journalism background, the *Rocky Mountain News* had asked Rivers to write "A Rookie's Diary" column when he was a free-agent fullback trying out for the Denver Broncos in 1991. His editor described his copy as "great ... really funny, well-written and grammatically correct" and told the Newspaper Fund that "if his football career ended, he could certainly get a job as a journalist." And so he did.

EXPANDING THE
EDITING PROGRAM

The editing program received a record 786 applications in 1991, the last full year of Engleman's tenure as executive director. Only 339 applications were received the previous year. Two major changes in the eligibility rules produced the increase. Seniors were allowed to apply, and graduate students who were minorities were included.

The Newspaper Fund mailed more than 23,000 application forms; eventually, 1,204 editing tests were mailed to editing professors proctoring the exams.

In 1991, *The Quill* magazine ranked the Newspaper Fund's editing internship program among the nation's best. Giles Fowler, an Iowa State University associate professor, surveyed 26 teachers or placement directors at journalism schools and asked them to nominate the nation's best internships. The result was 64 programs, with 17 making "a short list with three or more endorsements." Most programs cited were operated by individual newspapers, including *Newsday, The Oregonian, Chicago Tribune,* and *Los Angeles Times.*

The article also found, "For sheer intensity, nothing beats the two-week editing 'boot camp' endured by Dow Jones Fund editing interns before they report to their summer jobs."

Trayes, who has run at least one training program every year since 1968, believes there is no one formula for running a successful program. "It's never the same, and you don't do it the same way twice," he said. "The personalities, the newspapers that are served, what's going on in the world, the changes in the newspaper business, all change. It's a very dynamic enterprise."

In placing interns, matchmaking was key. Crutchfield noted that newspapers had certain needs for interns. "Demands of *The Washington Post* are different from *The Tampa Tribune,* for example," he said.

Daryl Frazell, who co-directed the editing residency at the University of Nebraska in the 1990s with Dick Thien and later with Charlyne Berens, agreed. "We try to match skills with needs," he said. "We meet the newspapers' geographic preferences, if any."

For example, newspapers such as *The Virginian-Pilot* in Norfolk, which in 2007 employed 12 former Newspaper Fund interns, prefers an intern from its state or region.

Ottaway Newspapers Inc., a subsidiary of Dow Jones, helped significantly expand the editing program in 1993. It was the first community newspaper group to work with the Newspaper Fund to set up its own training site. David Brace, then vice president for news at Ottaway, was looking for a way to attract minorities to the staff and college students to community newspapers.

The answer was the Newspaper Fund. Trayes directed the new program, assisted by Ottaway editors. Ottaway had Associated Press equipment installed to deliver digitized photographs at Temple so students could learn how to crop them. The interns also visited an Ottaway newsroom. "When our student interns joined our copy desks for 10 weeks in the summer, we regarded them as 'professionals' at community newspapers, and that's how they carried themselves," Brace said.

The Newspaper Fund returned to Nebraska in 1994, when a fifth residency was established. Thien and Frazell directed Nebraska's editing program the second time around.

"We used to say we were among the top 10 programs in the nation," Thien said shortly afterward. "No more. We take a back seat to no one – and that's because being a part of the Dow Jones Newspaper Fund has allowed us to raise standards. It has been terrific for the students and for the faculty."

At Nebraska, professionals instructed interns in editing, layout and headline writing during the first week, with the college faculty taking over the second week. Anne Glover, then assistant managing editor/copy desks at the *St. Petersburg Times* and a previous Newspaper Fund editing intern, was among the professionals who helped Thien and Frazell.

"Dow Jones editing students accept nothing at face value," Thien said. "They challenge, they question, they ask why and then ask why not. It lets us feel what it's like to be at an All-Star game. Every student is a star. It's a privilege for us to sit on the bench."

Of course, Thien and Frazell were hardly the type to ride the pine.

Thien was a University of Missouri journalism graduate, a founding editor of *USA Today* and an editor of award-winning Gannett newspapers, including the *Chronicle-Tribune* in Marion, Ind., and the *Argus Leader*, in Sioux Falls, S.D. He taught journalism at the State University of New York-Binghamton, at Nebraska and at the University of Kansas. He later became a writing and editing coach for the Freedom Forum's Chips Quinn Scholars Program.

Frazell taught reporting and editing as a visiting journalist in residence at the University of Kansas. With both an undergraduate and a graduate degree in journalism from Northwestern University, Frazell worked at news organizations with high standards. He started as a reporter for the legendary City News Bureau of Chicago. He worked as an editor for *The Minneapolis Star* and *Detroit Free Press*, as an assistant news editor for *The New York Times* and as an editor for the *St. Petersburg Times*. His textbook *Principles of Editing*, co-written with Nebraska colleague George Tuck, was published in 1996 and became widely used in journalism schools. Frazell retired in 2003.

Among the editing interns who trained at the 1993 Nebraska residency was Zoe Cabaniss Friloux, who interned at the *Argus Leader* in Sioux Falls. She worked as a copy editor at newspapers in Nashville and Phoenix before taking a job on the desk at the *Rocky Mountain News* in Denver. Cabaniss Friloux also studied editing with Rich Holden, the current executive director of the Newspaper Fund, on a fellowship at the Robert C. Maynard Institute for Journalism Education's Editing Program. She was an officer of the American Copy Editors Society before taking a leave in 2007.

SWENSSON'S LONG SHADOW

Swensson, who remained a Newspaper Fund director until he died in 2001, continued to exert influence well after he left.

He was disappointed with the Newspaper Fund's self-effacement and low profile. In 1982, he lamented the board's decision not to hold a reception on its 25th birthday. He wrote Engleman: "I wish that I could understand the reluctance of the board majority to be seen publicly in the company of those they have helped so wisely and generously. Maybe it is a deeply ingrained policy that predates even Barney Kilgore. Maybe it is the ultimate modesty and corporate self-protection."

Not long after Swensson's note, things began to change.

A quarter-century after its founding as The Newspaper Fund Inc., the organization's 1982 annual report quietly noted a name change. "The Dow Jones Newspaper Fund, as the name suggests, is an offspring of Dow Jones & Co. Inc., best known as the publisher of *The Wall Street Journal*. Most of the Fund's money is contributed by the company."

Reaction was mixed. The culture of Dow Jones long reflected the Midwest modesty of Barney Kilgore and others. Unduly promoting the company's name in its charitable efforts had been regarded as unseemly.

Trayes was among those who did not like the name change. "That wasn't the spirit of it," he said. "The name 'The Newspaper Fund' was OK with Kilgore and all of his people at the start of it all. It was there to help all newspapers, anywhere, all sizes. But this branded it."

Also in 1982, Swensson inquired about a proposed report on what makes a good editor. "If such a report were produced as a pamphlet, it might help editing teachers improve their course outlines," he wrote. "It might be the basis for advance courses in editing."

Always the teacher, Swensson appended to the note his view of what makes a good editor:

1) A master craftsman of our language.
2) A generalist on 20th century current affairs and common interests.
3) A specialist in several areas of knowledge and experience.
4) A hybrid who builds a pair of specialties on his generalist floor of knowledge and experience.
5) An expert on readership with keen understanding of what readers will read most of the time, sometimes and never. He knows how to influence readership of news that leads to decision-making by the readers.
6) An occasional volunteer as the conscience of the community.

7) A planner of predictable news which can be anticipated and scheduled.
8) A planner for the unscheduled but predictable news.
9) An advanced student of changes in newspaper technology.
10) A leader who can sell his news ideas to management.
11) A leader who teaches his staff and stimulates individuals to outdo themselves.
12) A humble person despite this wealth of talent and power.

Engleman described Swensson as "a teacher of teachers and a teacher of leaders."

ENGLEMAN AND THE ELECTRONIC ERA

In Princeton, Engleman was upgrading the Newspaper Fund's technology. When the first Apple Macintosh personal computer with page-design software became available, Engleman convinced Warren Phillips that it would pay for itself. With the Mac, Engleman could prepare camera-ready pages for the Newspaper Fund's literature. Fred Taylor, managing editor of *The Wall Street Journal*, sent one of his production editors to the Newspaper Fund's Princeton office to check it out. Not long after, more production-efficient computers were introduced at the *Journal*.

Engleman worked with the company's computer programmers to create a searchable database that could be sold on a disk to high school guidance counselors and journalism teachers. The program allowed students to compare their preferences for a college (location, cost, difficulty of admission, available journalism majors, etc.) with the database.

Engleman was just as savvy in recruiting staff. One of his smartest moves was hiring Janice Schegel in 1974 as office manager. She retired three decades later as Jan Maressa and was loved and respected by all who came into contact with the Newspaper Fund. "I depended on Jan to keep things going in that office," Engleman recalled. "She ran that place so that we could focus on what needed to be done and not so much on the nuts-and-bolts, day-to-day business, which she handled so well."

He also hired Linda Waller Nelson as his assistant. She had approached the Newspaper Fund as a high school student seeking information about journalism programs and scholarships. She ended up enrolling at the University of Bridgeport in Connecticut. After graduating and moving through a succession of newspaper jobs, she was appointed city editor at the *Herald-Statesman* in Yonkers, near New York City.

Meanwhile, she had become active in the National Association of Black Journalists. At NABJ's annual convention in 1987, she learned of a job opening at the Newspaper Fund.

In 2008, Waller – now Linda Shockley and deputy director – had been at the Newspaper Fund for 20 years.

Holden said Shockley played an important role in every innovation over the past two decades. "Linda commands respect, with her knowledge and personality, of everyone in and out of Dow Jones. She has been instrumental in developing our enhanced Web site – moving it from the 20th century into the 21st."

Holden also noted her other communications skills. "Tom Engleman was responsible for bringing the Newspaper Fund into the electronic age. But Linda has brought us into the age of Twitter, You Tube, Facebook and MySpace and, as a result, is making us far more accessible and relevant to today's youth," Holden said.

Shockley did find one challenge when she began working in the Newspaper Fund office. "It was very quiet," she said with a laugh. "I was used to working with a staff of 20 very busy reporters, and here I was waiting for the phone to ring."

POWERS BEHIND THE FUND

Bill Kerby, Kilgore's successor, was president of the Newspaper Fund when Engleman became executive director. Kerby was followed as president by Ed Cony and Larry O'Donnell.

Cony joined the board in 1967 and was president from 1980 to 1988. He retired as vice president/news of Dow Jones after serving as executive editor and managing editor of the *Journal*. He won a Pulitzer Prize in 1961 for national affairs reporting for the

Journal. He was president of the American Society of Newspaper Editors for a few hours in April 1988. A few weeks before he was to have assumed the post, he announced that he had Alzheimer's disease and had decided not to take the position. But the ASNE board elected him anyway, then quickly accepted his resignation. He died in early 2000.

O'Donnell joined *The Wall Street Journal* as a reporter in 1958, the year the Newspaper Fund was created. He served as the bureau chief in Detroit before becoming assistant managing editor in 1974. O'Donnell became managing editor in 1977, and during his tenure the paper's news coverage expanded considerably and a second section was added.

O'Donnell's term as president of the Newspaper Fund, which ran from 1988 to 1993, was marked by his commitment to helping minority students. Even before joining the board, he was an active supporter of the minority reporting program. "The Newspaper Fund has never had as dedicated and energetic a president as Larry," Peter Kann, then chairman and chief executive of Dow Jones, said as O'Donnell stepped down from presiding over the board.

Throughout the Newspaper Fund's first 50 years, many Dow Jones executives served on the board of directors, bringing essential expertise to the organization.

The Revenue and Expenditure Control Act of 1968 required foundations to have independent, outside directors. In response, the Newspaper Fund began to add alumni and college journalism administrators to the board. The first was Pamela Hollie, a former intern who was a reporter in New York when she was elected in fall 1973. Other directors included Jay Harris, a Gannett (and later Knight-Ridder) news executive who was an assistant dean at the Medill School of Journalism when he joined the board; Frank del Olmo, a 1969 reporting intern who rose to prominence at the *Los Angeles Times*; and Sharon Murphy, a Newspaper Fund Teacher Fellow who became dean of the College of Journalism at Marquette University and an expert on diversity issues.

Two other alumnae eventually were appointed to the board. Wanda Lloyd was an editing intern at the *Providence Evening Bulletin* in 1970 after training at Temple and was a senior editor of *USA*

Today. Barbara Martinez won a $1,000 scholarship through the minority reporting intern program in 1990 and was a Newspaper Fund editing intern at *The Wall Street Journal* in 1991. She was appointed graduate adviser to the board, a new position created to bring the perspective of a recent student to discussions. She later became a director and the Newspaper Fund's secretary.

END OF THE ENGLEMAN ERA

Engleman stepped down as executive director of the Newspaper Fund in 1992. "It was an amicable departure," he said. He left to become associate dean and director of development and alumni affairs in Temple University's School of Communications and Theater. He left that job in 1995, returning to Dow Jones as a database writer for its News/Retrieval Service.

Kann and O'Donnell expressed their appreciation for the job Engleman had done at the Newspaper Fund for 25 years. "Dozens of people within Dow Jones and hundreds of people outside of it got their start in journalism through the Newspaper Fund with Tom's help," they said.

6

RICH HOLDEN:
THE FUTURE IS NOW

Richard S. Holden succeeded Engleman in October 1992 as executive director of the Newspaper Fund. At the same time, Linda Shockley, who had been hired in 1988 as assistant to the director, was promoted to deputy director.

Holden, a 19-year veteran of *The Wall Street Journal*, was the newspaper's senior editor overseeing the hiring and training of editors. Prior to that he was the paper's financial editor.

Then Dow Jones Chairman Peter Kann and Larry O'Donnell, president of the Newspaper Fund, said they were "particularly pleased that one of *The Wall Street Journal*'s most senior news people has assumed the leadership of the Newspaper Fund."

The selection of Holden broke with the tradition since 1959 of hiring outsiders to direct the Newspaper Fund. Don Carter, Paul Swensson and Tom Engleman were not Dow Jones employees. Carter, who has been involved with the Newspaper Fund since its inception, commented: "I think this guy (Holden) you've got now is so much better than anyone who's ever filled the seat."

Kann and O'Donnell also hailed Holden's commitment to training young journalists and his leadership "in creating opportunities for minorities in *The Wall Street Journal* newsroom and elsewhere." His editing staff, they noted, was among "the most diverse at Dow Jones." Holden had also been teaching minority journalists and other professionals for a decade in the editing program of the Robert C. Maynard Institute for Journalism Education.

Holden earned his bachelor's and master's degrees in journalism at the University of Missouri, where he subsequently served as an adjunct professor. He joined the *Journal* as a copyreader in 1973 and later taught journalism at the Chinese University of Hong Kong while an editor on *The Asian Wall Street Journal* from 1976 through mid-1979.

Holden had other relevant experience for the job. As copy chief at the *Journal*, he had supervised several "uniformly excellent" Newspaper Fund editors and hired at least a half-dozen for full-time work. "I had always looked to have a Newspaper Fund intern work for me in the summers," Holden recalled. "I used to be a customer and here I am running it," he said. He believes that every graduate of the editing intern program "should have a shot at full-time employment at the end of the summer."

Holden articulated his vision for the Newspaper Fund in the fall 1992 issue of *AlumniNewsline*. He described the Newspaper Fund as a vital connection between J-schools and newspapers. "It's like building a bridge starting in the middle of the river, linking what the universities offer to what the industry needs and wants," Holden said.

He also pointed to the beginnings of rapid change in the way newspapers were evolving. New jobs, he predicted, would not be with traditional newspapers but with spinoffs such as fax editions, electronic information services and data retrieval. "The need will be for speed, speed, speed," he said. Holden wanted the editing intern program to train editors to use electronic systems expertly, including emerging electronic retrieval systems, layout and graphics applications.

He also wanted to expand the editing program. In the year he started, 642 students applied for 45 positions. Within a decade, applications would reach 800 annually, and the number of internships available would exceed 100.

The board faced a heavy agenda at its fall 1993 meeting. *Journal* Executive Washington Editor Albert R. Hunt was nominated and elected as president of the board, succeeding O'Donnell. Several new college programs were approved and funded for the next summer: a real-time information pilot project for student interns, an editing intern residency at Nebraska, an online editing internship program at the University of Missouri and an editing fellowship for journalism teachers at historically black colleges and universities.

The Newspaper Fund launched the real-time information project in the summer of 1994. Funded by a $5,000 grant, the program trained seven students in line editing, rewriting and newsroom ethics. The emphasis was on speed and newsroom technology.

The program was coordinated by Dr. Russell G. Todd of the University of Texas. He was assisted by Holden and Everett Groseclose, managing editor of the *Dow Jones Emerging Markets Report*, who was also vice president and secretary of the board.

One of the high-achieving graduates of the intern program was Christopher Kraeuter, who interned in 1998 at *Emerging Markets Report*. After graduating in 1999, he went to work as a business reporter for the San Francisco *Business Times*. In 2007, he was a senior technology reporter in San Francisco for Forbes.com.

Throughout the 1990s, under Holden's leadership, the Newspaper Fund sought ways to encourage more minority students to pursue careers as journalists. On its 25th anniversary in 1993, the Urban Journalism Workshops attracted 523 high schools students. The number was about 500 for the next few years.

The Newspaper Fund also sponsored a lunch at the Unity '94 convention of the minority journalism organizations in Atlanta, featuring Dr. Johnetta Cole, the president of Spelman College, as the speaker.

Urban Journalism Workshop students from Clark Atlanta University and Rider University in New Jersey attended the convention through Newspaper Fund support. The Rider students covered the convention for their workshop paper, assisted by

O'Donnell. The Newspaper Fund also offered skills workshops. Among the instructors was Phil Avila, a *Journal* copy editor who would join the Newspaper Fund staff years later.

That year, it added a four-day seminar on the teaching of copy editing for seven professors from historically black colleges and universities. The program focused on sharpening their editing and headline-writing skills and helping them teach students how to better prepare resumes and handle job interviews.

The Newspaper Fund revamped and reinvigorated another program for 1995, offering business reporting internships. It was under the direction of Barbara Martinez, an alumna and board member as well as a reporter for *The Wall Street Journal*. She was joined by Prof. Linda Steiner of Rutgers University and *Journal* reporters and editors during a five-day training course. Students who completed the internship successfully received a $1,000 scholarship. The program was run at Rutgers for two years before moving to New York University, where *Journal* reporter Lisa Brownlee assisted with instruction.

On the Newspaper Fund's 40th anniversary in 1998, board president Hunt reported that Our Lady of Good Counsel High School in Newark, N.J., had published five editions of the school paper with the "invaluable assistance" of the *Journal's* Martinez and Tim Layer. The predominantly minority student body at Good Counsel didn't have a student paper before that Newspaper Fund initiative. "Unfortunately," Hunt wrote, "this is not uncommon in inner-city schools. At least 15% of urban high schools don't have a newspaper. Many others publish only sporadically. In big cities like Chicago and Baltimore, half of the schools are without a paper." The Newspaper Fund's hope, he added, was to expand the Newark project and help several other urban high schools to launch papers.

Hunt also cited a study by Dr. Reginald Owens, then a Grambling State University journalism professor and member of the Newspaper Fund's board, who found that 25 of the nation's 118 historically black colleges had no student paper, and that of the rest, 18 had publications that were infrequent or sporadic.

In the 1998 annual report, Holden wrote: "We at the Newspaper Fund remain strongly committed to diversity in

American journalism, and we believe that close ties with the nation's historically black colleges are essential for that diversity to be achieved. It's essential that students of color are made aware of the opportunities that newspaper journalism presents. For us, the process begins with the Urban Journalism Workshops for high school students that we sponsor nationwide every summer. It continues as the students who attend these workshops go on to college, many at historically black institutions."

Back in 1978, the American Society of Newspaper Editors adopted an ambitious Year 2000 goal, challenging editors to shape newsroom staffs that were as diverse as the populations they served.

Jay Harris initiated ASNE's annual census of minority employment at daily papers, which has remained the industry benchmark. In 1978, minorities represented 4% of newsroom professionals. Although newsroom staffing had reached 11.46% minorities by 1998, the national population was 26%. ASNE recommitted itself with a new goal for 2025: doubling the minority staff in America's newsrooms to about 23%. The nation's minority population was expected to grow to about 38% by then.

The July 31, 2003, edition of *Black Issues in Higher Education* lamented the failure of the newspaper industry's minority hiring initiatives. ASNE had released its annual survey of minority journalists, showing little positive change from the previous year. There was an increase of just 40 black journalists, or 0.04%, at newspapers nationwide, after two years of decline. Minorities held just 12.5% of all newspaper jobs, the survey found.

THE LAWSUIT

After decades of encouraging minority students to consider careers in journalism, the Newspaper Fund faced a serious legal challenge in 2006. In September, a class-action lawsuit was filed by the Center for Individual Rights, a nonprofit public-interest law firm based in Washington, D.C., on behalf of a teenage girl who asserted that she was rejected for a Newspaper Fund program because she was white.

Emily Smith, 16, said she was accepted in the spring of

2006 to a summer Urban Journalism Workshop at Virginia Commonwealth University and then rejected a week later after organizers learned that she wasn't a minority.

The Newspaper Fund and the other principals agreed to a settlement, announced in February 2007, in which the lawsuit was withdrawn and neither the Newspaper Fund nor VCU admitted any wrongdoing. The Newspaper Fund agreed not to use race as a criteria for enrollment in its Urban Journalism Workshops and to acknowledge publicly that it would offer no preferential treatment or discriminate against any prospect "on the basis of race or ethnicity." In a statement, Dow Jones said: "The settlement is consistent with the longtime intent and practice of the Dow Jones Newspaper Fund to encourage young people of all races, cultures and physical abilities to be successful journalists."

VCU agreed to pay $25,000 to Smith and her attorneys and to admit her in the future but said the program would not change. "The program will continue, and race-neutral criteria will be used by VCU in the selection of participants," said Ray Kozakewicz, spokesman for Media General Inc., which publishes the *Richmond Times-Dispatch* and was a sponsor of the VCU program.

THE ECONOMIC FACTOR

In 1999, Dow Jones increased its contribution to the Newspaper Fund by $25,000, to $475,000, and again in 2000 to $500,000.

Much changed for the Newspaper Fund in 2001 after the Sept. 11 terrorist attacks. As the economy slumped over the next two years, the Newspaper Fund's budget was significantly reduced. Still, Holden was determined to preserve the flagship editing program and the business reporting program. In these circumstances, however, he was forced to suspend the real-time and online editing programs. In 2001, those programs provided internships for 24 students combined, nearly a fifth of the 110 total internships.

Holden was able to revive the online residency in 2007 at Western Kentucky University with the help of Yahoo!News, and the program thrived again. Holden also negotiated a new sports copy editing program in cooperation with Associated Press Sports Editors in 2003.

Overall, the number of interns in college programs tripled during the Holden years. Through 2008, the Newspaper Fund was able to provide at least 100 college internships each summer despite a host of problems.

The 2006 sale and breakup of Knight-Ridder alone eliminated about 30 internships. And the financial crisis in the newspaper industry, fueled by a combination of a severe recession and the effects of the Internet, forced sharp staff cutbacks, frequently involving interns.

With the assistance of Deputy Director Shockley and Project Manager Avila, a former *Journal* copy editor, Holden kept up dozens of other initiatives and programs that had been imagined and implemented by his predecessors. The high school journalism programs, for instance, were still going strong, and many of the publications that the Newspaper Fund produced or distributed were being moved to the Web. "These are the smaller, hidden jewels not everyone knows about," Holden said. "But they are a big part of what the Newspaper Fund is and always has been."

There were conventions and conferences to attend and relationships to cultivate and nurture, some of which had been established decades earlier and which required attention. Holden and Shockley maintained memberships in a number of professional associations including the College Media Advisers, Association for Education in Journalism and Mass Communication, American Copy Editors Society and the major minority journalism associations.

Through the years, Shockley has become increasingly active and has taken on a higher profile at conventions and conferences. She was on the Newspaper Fund staff for five years when Holden succeeded Engleman as executive director. "Rich came along, and he was known as a newspaper guy," Shockley recalled. "He didn't know a lot about scholastic journalism, which was the area where I was working the most, along with all the publications. His focus was on editing, and he has been determined to grow the editing program. In a way, he is not unlike Paul Swensson, who used his strong relationship with editors around the country to build things."

Holden and Shockley worked well as a team, complementing each other. "I could not, would not want to do this without Linda," Holden said. "She's the glue that holds us together."

Holden and Shockley, as a team, have worked under three presidents: Hunt (1993-2004), Byron Calame (2004-05), and Levine (since 2005).

Hunt was executive Washington editor of *The Wall Street Journal* when he was nominated and elected president of the Newspaper Fund board. Like his predecessors, Hunt was a Dow Jones insider. But for the first time since Barney Kilgore held the post, Hunt was a new kind of face for the Newspaper Fund. As Peter Kann noted, Hunt is "an extraordinarily distinguished" and "widely recognized" journalist.

He joined the *Journal* in 1965 as a reporter in New York and moved to Boston before arriving at the Washington bureau in 1969. He covered Congress and national politics from 1972 until 1983 when he was named Washington bureau chief. He also moderated CNN's weekly *Capital Gang* program and appeared frequently on NBC's *Today* and *Meet the Press* shows.

Calame was a much-honored journalist who retired as deputy managing editor of the *Journal* and became president briefly in late 2004. He left the Newspaper Fund within months to become the second public editor at *The New York Times*.

He joined the Journal in 1965 and worked in New York, Los Angeles and Washington, D.C., before becoming a bureau chief in Pittsburgh. He returned to Los Angeles as bureau chief in 1978 and returned to New York as a senior editor in 1987. He was named deputy managing editor in 1992, charged with, among other duties, maintaining and monitoring reporting and ethical standards.

RICHARD J. LEVINE:
FROM INTERN TO PRESIDENT

In Dick Levine, who succeeded Calame, the Newspaper Fund got a much more hands-on president than any of his predecessors, though O'Donnell had been deeply involved in recruiting minority journalists during his tenure as president.

Levine entered Cornell University in Ithaca, N.Y., as

a freshman in the fall of 1958. The Ivy League school had no journalism program, but it did have an independent daily student newspaper, the *Cornell Daily Sun*. Levine went to work on the paper immediately and was elected sports editor as a sophomore and managing editor as a junior.

In the spring of his sophomore year, he heard about a new internship program sponsored by the Newspaper Fund through *The Wall Street Journal*. When he applied, Don Carter told him all the internships had been awarded but that he could have a scholarship if he could find a summer newspaper job on his own. Levine found his chance on *The Ithaca Journal*, the afternoon newspaper in his college town.

As an undergraduate, Levine's journalism education consisted of self-tutoring on the *Sun* and the Newspaper Fund internship. "I began to master the basics of news reporting, writing and analysis. I was not a great student in the traditional sense but I worked hard in the newsroom." Levine recalled. "I really majored in the *Cornell Daily Sun*."

During college, Levine made some important contacts at Dow Jones. Not only had he completed a Newspaper Fund reporting internship during the first year of the program, but he had interviewed with Ed Cony, managing editor of *The Wall Street Journal*, when he was recruiting at Cornell. As he was completing a two-year tour as an Army lieutenant, he wrote Cony inquiring about job possibilities. Levine was hired by the *Journal* as a general assignment reporter in the Washington bureau. While based there from 1966 to 1980, he covered the White House, organized labor, military and economic affairs, reporting from around the U.S. and overseas much of the time.

"I spent 15 years in the greatest jobs the craft had to offer, and had a front-row seat to some of the biggest stories of the last third of the 20th century," he recalled. In 1980, he moved into management as the editorial director of a small team tasked with starting an electronic publishing division for Dow Jones. He claimed no technical proficiency but became intrigued by opportunities as Dow Jones moved into new distribution technologies.

In 1987, Levine was promoted to vice president of the Information Services Group, with responsibility for guiding the commercial, technical and editorial operations of Dow Jones News/Retrieval and DowPhone. From 1989 to 1992, he served as vice president and editorial director of Information Services, overseeing the group's domestic editorial operations, product development and business operations. From 1992 to 1995, he served as vice president and managing editor of Dow Jones Information Services. He was vice president and managing editor and then executive editor of Dow Jones Newswires from 1995 to 2005, when he was named vice president of news and staff development for Dow Jones.

In 2005, after Calame's sudden resignation as president of the Newspaper Fund, Levine was approaching retirement age. He crossed paths with Peter Kann, then Dow Jones chairman and chief executive who was looking for a successor to Calame and wondered whether Levine was interested in the job.

The decision was easy, Levine said. "It was something I cared deeply about because it was so important to the start of my career in journalism. I instantly sensed that this was something I could sink my teeth into." He accepted on the spot. "I just said, 'I'll do it,' " Levine recalled, adding with a laugh: "So I have Barney Calame to thank for this job."

In announcing Levine's appointment, Kann said: "Dick is an outstanding choice for this position. As an intern himself at the Fund during his college years, Dick appreciates the Fund's importance in attracting people to, and helping them prepare for, careers in journalism."

In retirement, Levine has had more time to devote to the Newspaper Fund. His tenure quickly became an exercise in dealing with several challenges: a drop in newspaper participation in the internship programs; the lawsuit involving a diversity workshop in Virginia; the newspaper industry's deepening economic crisis in the face of new competition for readers and advertisers from the Internet and the worst recession since the Great Depression; the growing need for multimedia skills in the nation's newsrooms and the initial uncertainty arising from the acquisition of Dow Jones by Rupert Murdoch's News Corp. in 2007.

News Corp.'s purchase of Dow Jones posed a challenge – the prospect of operating in a new corporate culture. News Corp.'s holdings included the *New York Post* as well as *The Times of London* and Fox News. To many observers the pairing of Dow Jones and News Corp. seemed awkward, and they expressed concern about the effect on Dow Jones's commitment to quality journalism.

Levine and Holden, however, have consistently maintained that under Murdoch the Newspaper Fund's future could be brighter than ever. At the 2007 meeting to select the new interns, Levine proclaimed his faith in the Newspaper Fund's future, citing passages from Murdoch's May 14, 2007, letter to the Bancroft family expressing his initial interest in purchasing Dow Jones and committing to increased funding for the Dow Jones Foundation, the primary beneficiary of which had long been the Newspaper Fund.

Levine knew something about philanthropy. When he received the Newspaper Fund scholarship after successfully completing his reporting internship in 1960, the $500 check was mailed to his parents' home that autumn. His father took the check and promptly invested it on his son's behalf in Esso stock. There it sat for decades, until Levine's accountant suggested he use the appreciated stock to make gifts to good causes. The investment had grown to "tens of thousands of dollars," Levine said. He used it to make donations to Cornell and to various cultural organizations.

Holden said he maintains an excellent relationship with Levine and the board. "The board has very little involvement in the day-to-day work of the Dow Jones Newspaper Fund," he said. "A number of the members are non-Dow Jones employees. They meet once a year, listen to recommendations, occasionally make some of their own, and that can be really valuable because you get all kinds of perspectives and insights. Ultimately, it's my job to propose programming and budgets, and they vote whether to approve or not."

In 2009, the longest-serving outside directors, who joined the board in 1996, were Profs. Rusty Todd and Reginald Owens.

Todd had been a news editor for *The Asian Wall Street Journal* and the first editor of the *Dow Jones Emerging Markets Report.* When he joined the board, he held the G.B. Dealey Chair in the journalism department at the University of Texas-Austin. Todd has long been active as a director or guest instructor in various Newspaper Fund residencies and workshops, particularly relating to business.

Owens at the time was an associate professor at Grambling State University and a leading scholar on the African-American press. He currently holds the F.J. Taylor endowed chair of journalism at Louisiana Tech University.

In November 2007, the Newspaper Fund elected two senior Dow Jones news executives to the board: Neal Lipschutz, senior vice president and managing editor of *Dow Jones Newswires*, and Cathy Panagoulias, then an assistant managing editor at the *Journal*. Lipschutz joined Dow Jones in 1982 as a copyreader for *Capital Markets Report* and had risen through the company ranks. Panagoulias, at the time of her election, was responsible for recruiting editors and reporters for the *Journal* and ran the college intern program. Like Holden, she had worked on *The Asian Wall Street Journal's* copy desk in Hong Kong.

They joined a board that included Peter Kann, retired chairman and chief executive officer of Dow Jones; Robin Gibson Sawyer, 2000 National High School Journalism Teacher of the Year; Diana Mitsu-Klos, senior project director, American Society of Newspaper Editors; Don Carter, first executive director; Melanie Kirkpatrick, deputy editorial page editor, *The Wall Street Journal*; Tom Engleman, New Jersey Press Foundation; Larry O'Donnell, retired managing editor of *The Wall Street Journal*; James H. Ottaway Jr., retired president/chief executive, Ottaway Newspapers Inc.; and Holden, executive director.

Early in 2008, there were two more additions to the board that signaled the support of the new News Corp. ownership – Leslie Hinton, chief executive officer of Dow Jones, publisher of *The Wall Street Journal*, and a long-time colleague of Murdoch, and Gregory Giangrande, senior vice president and chief human resources officer of Dow Jones.

THE RESIDENCY DIRECTORS

As the editing intern program expanded under Holden's watch, alumni became increasingly connected. He credited the professors who were running the residencies. While giving them free rein over what they teach and how, he expected them to stay in touch with past interns.

Trayes's lasting influence on his Newspaper Fund interns – his "NFI's" as he calls them – reflects that commitment.

Take 1997, for instance. On May 16 of that year, he walked into the Diamond Club at Temple to find more than 50 of his former "NFIs" applauding him for 30 summers of training. "Ed's former interns don't look at him as just some nostalgic figure from long ago when they struggled to learn copy editing from him in two weeks," Deputy Director Shockley said in an interview. "They stay in touch with him. They always have. They ask him for career advice, they tell him what's going on in their personal lives, if they get married or have babies."

At the gathering, Richard Fausset, who trained at the residency in 1996, recalled "squinting, at 2:30 a.m., at the part of the Stylebook that bothers to illuminate the pedantic and obscure difference between a 'pom-pom' and a 'pompon' in a neon-lit dorm room on a Philadelphia Saturday night amidst the sounds of gun play and auto alarms, for sure. But … [doing it] out of respect for a teacher whose curriculum extends far beyond the matter at hand." Said Trayes: "Those 12 days, they live and breathe journalism. It's not just about copy editing. It's about them as people."

Kim Kavin of the class of 1994 described the "flailing" episode that year. During the stylebook quiz, the interns swung their arms wildly above their heads when Trayes, seeking a definition or usage in a sentence, called out the word "flail." Kavin recalled: "Dr. Trayes looked up, stunned …. The students continued for mere moments. But the victory of a lifetime was theirs. Suppressing a giggle and desperately shrouding his surprise. Dr. Trayes continued: 'Question 37….'"

Amy Wang, then a deputy editor at *Philadelphia Inquirer Magazine,* began planning the event nearly a year earlier. She was an intern in 1990 and was invited to return in 1993 to be the "house mom" looking after the interns. She then understood the extent to which Trayes always went "beyond the call of duty for 'his' kids."

Trayes told the group: "We've got so much talent in this room, we could put out a newspaper!"

Then there was the surprise from the Temple residency class of 1979 on its 25th anniversary in 2004.

"Nothing beats the class of 1979," Trayes said in an interview. "I couldn't believe it!" Every one of Trayes's interns from 1979 showed up on a Saturday morning. The alumni walked into his classroom in unison, surprising Trayes and raising his ire for disrupting a lesson. They refused to leave the room. "Each one stood behind the chair of one of the new interns," he recalled.

The 1979 group had one more surprise for Trayes – a $10,000 endowment to establish the Edward Trayes Scholarship. Each year, Trayes selects the top intern at the residency, who receives a $1,000 scholarship in addition to the one from the Newspaper Fund.

The scholarship was established by the O'Toole Family Foundation, headed by Terence M. O'Toole, who interned at *The Wall Street Journal*, and went on to become an executive with Goldman Sachs in New York City. "The fact that after a quarter of a century, all of his students would return on a Saturday is testimony to the impact that Ed had on our lives," O'Toole said.

Through the Temple editing residencies, he trained more than 500 interns in 40 years. "For me, it's always been about a lifetime of service to the profession," Trayes said. "Make it important to every student. This is an amazing privilege. Make the most of it."

He added: "I always try each year to bring back a few people who have gone through the program and made something of themselves. To bring a sense of tradition to the whole thing, to help them understand what this is all about, such as who has gone before them."

One such graduate was Juan Williams, who went through the residency when it lasted three weeks. Before he went to *The Washington Post* and then to National Public Radio and Fox News, Williams, a junior at Haverford College in 1975, spent the summer on the copy desk of the *Providence Journal* in Rhode Island.

Williams returned to Temple in October 2007 to give two lectures – "Eyes on the Prize: The Truths of American Racism," and "Thurgood Marshall: An American Revolutionary." Trayes recalled Williams as "quiet, very serious-minded," and in a post-summer 1975 evaluation projected Williams could achieve great things.

Brian Brooks's roots in the Newspaper Fund run deep, too. The 50th anniversary of the Newspaper Fund was Brooks's 32nd year working with the Newspaper Fund. Brooks co-founded the editing residency at the University of Missouri with Newspaper Fund alumnus Prof. Daryl Moen in 1976.

After serving in the Army, the Tennessee-born Brooks worked as a reporter, copy editor and night city editor at the *Memphis* (Tenn) *Press-Scimitar.* He joined Missouri's journalism faculty in 1974 as news editor of the *Missourian,* then became its editor for three years beginning in 1984. His work in information technologies on behalf of the school earned him notice. He helped bring in a $15 million grant from IBM Corp. from 1989 to 1997. Later, he helped lead the school through its switch to the Apple platform. In 2001, he was honored with an Apple Distinguished Educator national award.

Brooks's teaching influence extended beyond the Missouri campus and the Newspaper Fund program. He was author or co-author of four journalism textbooks, including the widely used *The Art of Editing.* After serving as chairman of the school's editorial department from 1999 until 2003, he became associate dean for undergraduate studies and administration. In addition to his work at Missouri, Brooks took a leave of absence to serve as the editor of the European edition of *Stars and Stripes.*

Typical of the high achievers who have thrived during Brooks's career at Missouri was Alyssa Appelman of St. Louis. She had a double major in journalism and French, studied in Australia during the summer of 2005 and helped edit an online magazine at Missouri. That fall, though only a sophomore, she was selected as an editing intern for *The Washington Times,* for which she trained at the University of Central Florida residency in May 2006.

"It definitely confirmed my decision to go into copy editing," Appelman said. She returned to Missouri for the fall semester, then spent spring and summer 2007 studying in Paris. In 2008, she received a summer internship at *The Washington Post.*

For most of three and a half decades, Missouri students

and Newspaper Fund interns have benefited from the instruction and influence of Brooks, who indicated that he may step down as director of the residency when he retires from Missouri. "I'd like to stay on for a few more years, maybe," he said. "I'm not sure who my successor would be. But I'd like to think the program should stay at Missouri."

Bill Tillinghast, John Clarke's graduate assistant at Ohio State, directed an editing intern residency at San Jose State University starting in 1985. He was a reporter at the *San Jose Mercury News*, *Columbus Dispatch*, and Lincoln (Neb.) *Evening Journal*.

Tillinghast and his wife, Diana Stover, who co-directed the San Jose State training program, jointly received the Trayes Award for Outstanding Contributions to the Mass Communication Field at the 1996 convention of the Association for Education in Journalism and Mass Communication. They had co-edited *Mass Comm Review*, an academic journal, since 1992. Stover had been solo editor for five years before that, with previous stints as guest editor and associate editor. Tillinghast was her associate editor from 1989 to 1991.

Charlyne Berens joined the University of Nebraska faculty full time in 1995 and assisted Frazell and Thien in teaching the residency there. She co-directed the program with Frazell, then took over in 2004, the second year of the sports editing intern program. Holden called it "an overwhelming success" and said the evaluations he received from sports desk supervisors were uniformly positive.

Berens was head of the news-editorial sequence at Nebraska. She taught junior high school English before spending 14 years as editor and co-publisher of a community newspaper in Seward, Neb. She helped produce *Renovating the Republic*, a magazine about Germany that was published in August 2007 by the depth reporting class that has been part of the Nebraska curriculum since the Newspaper Fund underwrote it as an experimental course in the 1960s. Berens has written several books, most recently *Chuck Hagel: Moving Forward*, a biography of Nebraska's recently retired U.S. senator.

S. Griffin "Griff" Singer, a retired senior lecturer at the University of Texas-Austin, has directed the intern training program there since it began in 1997.

In three decades of teaching at Texas, Singer taught reporting, copy editing, newspaper layout and design and computer-assisted reporting and sports reporting. He worked as a reporter or editor for three Texas newspapers and directed coverage for *The Dallas Morning News* of President Kennedy's assassination. He also was a consultant and part-time assistant metro editor at the *Houston Chronicle*.

At the Texas residency, Singer revived a tradition of having interns produce a newspaper. Singer's interns produced three editions of *The Southwest Journalist*, a six-page daily. Live stories and photos came from the Associated Press, and other copy was taken from *The Daily Texan* campus newspaper. "Many students have done work around the school copy desk," Singer said. "They really didn't understand how the paper was put together."

The operation was modeled after a typical daily, with story and photo budgets and morning and afternoon news meetings. Students assumed newsroom roles for the day. "We had a lot fun," Singer said. "We worked with realistic deadlines."

The online program, launched in 1996 and suspended after 2002, was restarted in 2007 thanks to a grant from Yahoo!News. Dr. Ann M. Brill directed the first series of workshops at the University of Missouri, where she taught for eight years and developed one of the world's first online newspapers, *The Digital Missourian*. She joined the faculty of the William Allen White School of Journalism and Mass Communications at the University of Kansas in 2000. In 2004, Brill was named the school's first female dean. She worked for newspapers in Wisconsin, Minnesota, and Montana.

It was a Newspaper Fund alumnus who would spearhead the online program's revival. Holden worked with Neil Budde, a 1976 Newspaper Fund intern at *The Charlotte Observer* who went on to senior management positions at Yahoo!News, to arrange a training program at Western Kentucky University, Budde's alma mater. "Yahoo!News is pleased to work with the Newspaper Fund to help prepare a future generation of online editors," said Budde, who now is an executive with the *DailyMe*. The first one-week training residency in Bowling Green, Ky., was led by Dr. Pam

Johnson, director of the School of Journalism and Broadcasting and the first black female publisher of a general circulation American newspaper, Gannett's *Ithaca* (N.Y.) *Journal.*

Penn State University joined the Newspaper Fund family in 2004. Holden had been considering Penn State for a residency when Ottaway Newspapers came back into the Newspaper Fund's fold with a proposal in 2003. The university had several pluses, chief among them Gene Foreman, a former managing editor of *The Philadelphia Inquirer.*

He was the university's Larry and Ellen Foster Professor of Communications and became the residency director. "Gene is truly an editor's editor," Holden noted in announcing the new residency, "and the students will benefit greatly from his many years of experience in the industry."

The program was bolstered with the addition of Dr. Marie Hardin, who arrived at Penn State in 2003. Foreman and Hardin were a strong team. The program also had the full support of Douglas Anderson, dean of the College of Communications.

"It was a tremendous opportunity to work with Gene on the program until he retired in 2006," said Hardin, who became the residency director. "I think the strength of our program is the array of Penn State and visiting faculty and editors who are involved," she said. "The faculty members from our large department are eager to contribute, which makes my job very easy."

With the addition of Ottaway, 2004 was a banner year for the Newspaper Fund, with 123 students receiving editing and reporting internships. The next year was even better, with 126 interns and trainees.

The University of North Carolina was one of two sites that trained Knight-Ridder interns in 2006; San Jose State was the other.

The sale of Knight-Ridder put the North Carolina program in jeopardy. But a new sponsor, Morris Communications of Augusta, Ga., partly filled the void. For 2007, Morris sponsored eight interns for the residency, which had been directed by Bill Cloud for eight years.

Cloud had been a professor at the university since 1982, teaching beginning and advanced classes in copy editing. He co-directed the Summer Institute for Midcareer Copy Editors at North Carolina. Sponsored by the Knight Foundation, the institute trained 18 editors each year. He also is a popular instructor in skills development workshops at American Copy Editors Society conventions. Cloud has been an editing coach at the *News & Record* in Greensboro, N.C., and *The News & Observer* in Raleigh. He came to North Carolina from *Newsday*, where he oversaw the features copy desk. Before working at *Newsday*, he was a reporter and copy editor at *The Miami Herald*. The Newspaper Fund editing residency at North Carolina was discontinued for 2008.

Succession planning for the directors of the residential workshops, management and the board looms. As Holden noted, "many of us, myself included, are getting on in years, and it's a matter of finding younger people to bring in. We need to address that in the not-too-distant future."

While conceding that much work remains to be done in many areas, he said he looks forward to the Newspaper Fund's next 50 years. "The newspaper industry is undergoing and will continue to undergo change. But if there's one factor that has remained constant over the past half-century, it's the Newspaper Fund's ability to spot changes and adapt our programs to meet industry needs."

EPILOGUE:
THE NEXT FIFTY YEARS

B arney Kilgore's determination 50 years ago to expose some of the nation's brightest students to newspaper work in the hope they would consider careers in journalism is as relevant today as it was then.

Journalism and journalists remain vital to providing Americans with the news and information they require to function as responsible citizens in the world's oldest democracy. While newspapers delivered on newsprint are clearly in decline and news will increasingly be delivered to readers electronically on a broad array of desktop and mobile devices, professional reporters and editors still will be required to produce objective, fact-based news.

Thus it is likely that newsroom managers will continue to look to the Newspaper Fund for the talent they require. In its first half-century, the Newspaper Fund offered more than 6,000 college students the highest quality training in editing and reporting. And it has helped educate tens of thousands of high school journalism teachers and publications advisers and their students about journalism.

It expects to continue this vital work long into the future, though the men and women who guide the Newspaper Fund today recognize they will be operating in a new and challenging environment. The crisis in the newspaper industry, still the largest employer of professional journalists, has taken a toll on the Newspaper Fund.

For one thing, buyouts and layoffs in the nation's newsrooms have eliminated jobs of senior editors who are former Newspaper Fund interns themselves or long-time supporters of the Newspaper Fund. Moreover, many of those who remain have smaller budgets and less freedom to hire interns each summer.

Joe Grimm, a highly regarded recruiter for the *Detroit Free Press*, accepted a buyout from his newspaper in July 2008. For years, Grimm had been a favorite with the Newspaper Fund, at times joining the residency directors in Princeton to assist in identifying top interns.

Merrill Perlman, director of copy desks at *The New York Times*, also accepted a buyout in 2008. Perlman had worked for years with Newspaper Fund interns trained by Ed Trayes at Temple. As she prepared to turn to consulting and recruiting, Perlman still believed in the Newspaper Fund's future. "I know what it offers, and I can't understand why other organizations don't participate," she said. The *Times* expanded its commitment in 2007 and 2008, employing as many as five Newspaper Fund copy editing interns.

"It's a commitment on the part of [managing editor] Jill Abramson, specifically, and the *Times*, in general," Perlman said. "It's an investment in the future."

Dick Levine spent much of his first three years as president of the Newspaper Fund planning for its future. As the 50th anniversary approached, Levine wrote, "Our aim is to strengthen our organization for its second half-century."

Toward that goal, a three-year strategic plan was developed for the first time. Top priorities were to strengthen the Newspaper Fund's board, secure the college internship program by providing expanded multimedia training and explore new sources of internships and funding, Holden said. Other goals were to improve how the Newspaper Fund worked with high school students and advisers, reconnect with former college interns and redesign and modernize its Web site. By 2008, considerable progress had been made.

As its 50th birthday approached, the Newspaper Fund received support from the industry that it had loyally served.

At its annual convention in Denver in April 2008, the American Copy Editors Society presented its first Hank Glamann Award, named after one of the society's co-founders, to the Newspaper Fund. Holden was absent that night because he was attending conventions of the American Society of Newspaper Editors and the Newspaper Association of America in Washington, D.C., Trayes accepted the award.

"The Dow Jones [Newspaper] Fund has generated hundreds, maybe thousands of quality copy editors over the years – a great many of whom stood up when called upon at Friday night's banquet," the ACES Web site said. "It was the vision of newspaper editors who believed in supporting generations of budding journalists and who believed in quality editing. It's a fine first recipient of the Glamann Award."

Some, including Holden, believe that smaller community newspapers and Internet-based news organizations will play a much larger role in the future than major metropolitan newspapers. That makes sense, given the greater financial strength of community papers and the growth rates of online publications.

"It's horrible that the Fund might be losing the bigger papers, but it's terrific to get the smaller papers involved," said Perlman, who started her career on a 35,000-circulation daily, the *Southern Illinoisian* in Carbondale.

But even if the big-city papers take fewer Newspaper Fund interns, they'll still benefit in the long run from its efforts to identify and train young journalists. After all, the first Newspaper Fund reporting interns in 1960 found summer work in towns like Ithaca and Keokuk and Quincy. Even more important, they found journalism, which many chose to make their life's work.

And that, above all, represents the fulfillment of Barney Kilgore's dream and the Dow Jones Newspaper Fund's crowning achievement in its first 50 years.

8

THE CALL

I got The Call in late December 1978 as a 19-year-old junior at Bethany College in West Virginia. I was alone and without light or heat in a dormitory long since closed for the winter. I was waiting a few more hours to finish a final exam I had missed because I'd found reading the campus newspaper's back issues more compelling than reading Ethan Frome. A quiet but sharp voice at the other end of the phone asked me about my interest in newspaper editing. I responded honestly because at the time I didn't know any other way.

I was a hungry college newspaper editor whose ambition had been fueled by the historic coverage of Watergate by *Washington Post* reporters Bob Woodward and Carl Bernstein. Answering in the affirmative to almost every question, I began to wonder whether I'd heard the caller's identity correctly at the beginning of our conversation. I asked testily whether he was trying to sell me something over the phone.

"I'm talking about the Newspaper Fund, goddamn it!" he growled. "Now, are you interested in a summer editing internship or not? I'm talking about sending you to *The Palm Beach Post*, goddamn it!"

And so I met Bill Turpin.

He was then the Southern region residency director for the Newspaper Fund at Virginia Commonwealth University in Richmond, where he would train me for two weeks before I began my editing internship in the summer of '79. Sending me off from Richmond when the course ended, he bear-hugged me and boomed, "You're off on the adventure of your life! Go get 'em, kid!"

And so I tried. I found more than just summer work at 10 newspapers over a quarter-century in journalism and teaching. I found my calling, thanks to The Call.

I was able to direct the Southern Center for Editing Excellence, the legacy of the late Turpin and the VCU program's administrator, George Crutchfield. I've had a chance to make The Call.

But I'm no Bill Turpin or George Crutchfield. They are legends of the Fund.

So are the Fund's four executive directors: Don E. Carter, Paul Swensson, Tom Engleman, Rich Holden.

And the Fund's presidents: Barney Kilgore, Bill Kerby, Ed Cony, Larry O'Donnell, Al Hunt, Barney Calame, Dick Levine.

And the many other residency directors over time: Ed Trayes, Jack Botts, Gene Gilmore, Larue Gilleland, Ted Conover, John Clarke, Brian Brooks, Daryl Moen, Daryl Frazell, Dick Thien, Bill Tillinghast, Diana Stover, Griff Singer, Rusty Todd, Charlyne Berens, Ann Brill, Gene Foreman, Marie Hardin, Pam Johnson and others.

And the tens of thousands of college interns, high school students, teachers and advisers who have shaped the history of the Newspaper Fund so far.

I'm just the former intern who has had the honor of writing their story.

9

ACKNOWLEDGMENTS

I am grateful in this endeavor for the help of many people: Rich Holden, Dick Levine, Linda Shockley, Phil Avila and Diane Cohn. Interviews with Don Carter, Ed Trayes and Tom Engleman proved invaluable. Bless their sharp memories, but more to the point, bless them for what they've done for the Newspaper Fund. I am grateful, too, for the many Newspaper Fund employees and officials whose memory and writing I have relied on in telling their story. The names of current and former Newspaper Fund directors, interns, teacher-fellows, and others are too many to list here, but they know who they are, and I hope they realize my debt to them.

Finally, I am also grateful for and proudest of my daughter, Zoe, who assisted in the research for this book. She is a bright and beautiful college student, a true wordsmith, and the same age I was when I was chosen as a Newspaper Fund intern. I hope that some day she, too, gets The Call and that she writes the history of the Newspaper Fund's next 50 years.

APPENDIX 1

Dow Jones Newspaper Fund National High School Journalism Teachers of the Year

2009   Paul Kandell, *Palo Alto (Calif.) Senior High School*
2008   Karl Grubaugh, *Granite Bay (Calif.) High School*
2007   Jim McGonnell, *Findlay (Ohio) High School*
2006   Alan Weintraut, *Annandale (Va.) High School*
2005   Linda Ballew, *Great Falls (Mont.) High School*
2004   Brenda Gorsuch, *West Henderson High School, Hendersonville, N.C.*
2003   Beth Fitts, *Oxford (Miss.) High School*
2002   Donald Bott, *Amos Alonzo Stagg High School, Stockton, Calif.*
2001   Terry Nelson, *Muncie (Ind.) Central High School*
2000   Robin Sawyer, *Manteo (N.C.) High School*
1999   Randy Swikle, *Johnsburg (Ill.) High School*
1998   Kathleen Zwiebel, *Pottsville (Pa.) Area High School*
1997   C. Dow Tate, *Hillcrest High School, Dallas*
1996   Merle Dieleman, *Pleasant Valley (Iowa) Community High School*
1995   Patricia S. Graff, *La Cueva High School, Albuquerque*

1994   Nick Ferentinos, *Homestead High School, Cupertino, Calif.*
1993   Jack Kennedy, *City High School, Iowa City*
1992   Gloria Grove Olman, *Utica (Mich.) High School*
1991   Carol Lange, *Thomas Jefferson High School for Science and Technology, Alexandria, Va.*
1990   Steve O'Donoghue, *The Media Academy at John C. Fremont High School, Oakland, Calif.*
1989   Candace Perkins Bowen, *St. Charles (Ill.) High School*
1988   Robert L. Button, *Grosse Pointe (Mich.) South High School*
1987   John Cutsinger, *Westlake High School, Austin*
       Jack Harkrider, *Anderson High School, Austin*
1986   Alyce Culpepper, *South Plantation High School, Plantation, Fla.*
1985   George Taylor, *Tamaqua (Pa.) Area High School*
1984   Rod Vahl, *Central High School, Davenport, Iowa*
1983   John Bowen, *Lakewood (Ohio) High School*
1982   Homer L. Hall, *Kirkwood (Mo.) High School*
1981   Wayne Brasler, *University High School, Chicago*
1980   Dr. Regis Boyle, *Walt Whitman High School, Bethesda, Md.*
1979   Jackie Engel, *McPherson (Kan.) High School*
1978   Col. Charles Savedge, *Augusta Military Academy, Fort Defiance, Va.*
1977   Ron Clemons, *Truman High School, Independence, Mo.*
1976   William Steinecke, Jr., *Frontier Regional School, S. Deerfield, Mich.*
1975   Christina Beeson-Bailey, *Colton (Calif.) High School*
1974   Randy Stano, *A.N. McCallum High School, Austin*
1973   Ronnie Hayes, *Lewiston (Idaho) High School*
1972   J. Brent Norlem, *Brooklyn Center (Minn.) High School*
1971   Ann Heintz, *St. Mary Center for Learning, Chicago*
1970   Elaine Pritchett, *Memorial Senior High School, Houston*
1969   Virginia Woodring, *School District of Springfield, Missouri*
1968   Ruth Marie Griggs, *Broad Ripple High School, Indianapolis*
1967   Mary Benedict, *Arlington High School, Indianapolis*
1966   Ralph Chavez, *Thomas Jefferson High School, El Paso*
1965   Dorry Coppoletta, *Oakland (Calif.) Technical High School*
1964   Jim Powell, *Carlsbad (N.M.) Senior High School*
1963   Opal Eckert, *Maryville (Mo.) High School*
1962   Dorothy Greer, *Topeka (Kan.) High School*
1961   Anthony L. Cassen, *Blair Academy, Blairstown, N.J.*
1960   Dr. William Nolan, *Harry Ellis High School, Richmond, Calif.*

APPENDIX 2

Members of the Board of Directors
1959 to Present

* President
**Executive Director

*Bernard Kilgore	*1959-1966*
Robert Bottorff	*1959-1970*
*William Kerby	*1959-1980*
Buren McCormack	*1959-1972*
Vermont Royster	*1959-1970*
**Don Carter	*1959-present*
**Paul Swensson	*1962-2001*
Warren Phillips	*1966-1991*
* Ed Cony	*1967-1999*
**Thomas Engleman	*1970-present*
William Giles	*1971-1978*
Charles Smith	*1972-1984*

Pamela Hollie	*1973-1974*
Frederick Taylor	*1973-1989*
Ruth Ann Hlavacek	*1976-1977*
Everett Groseclose	*1976-1998*
Jay Harris	*1979-1989*
Linda Martelli	*1978-1985*
Betty Duval	*1981-1991*
*Larry O'Donnell	*1985-present*
Tom Sullivan	*1985-2004*
Frank del Olmo	*1986-1992*
Sharon Murphy	*1986-1995*
Don Miller	*1989-1999*
Robert Bartley	*1991-1997*
Norman Pearlstine	*1991-1992*
**Richard Holden	*1992-present*
Peter Kann	*1992-present*
Wanda Lloyd	*1992-1999*
Barbara Martinez	*1992-present*
*Albert Hunt	*1993-2004*
Reginald Owens	*1996-present*
Russell Todd	*1996-present*
Melanie Kirkpatrick	*1998-2008*
Fernando Dovalina	*2000-2002*
Vickee Adams	*2000-2006*
Robin Sawyer	*2001-present*
*Byron Calame	*2004-2005*
James Ottaway	*2004-2008*
*Richard Levine	*2005-present*
Diana Mitsu-Klos	*2005-present*
Thomas McGuirl	*2005-2008*
Cathy Panagoulias	*2007-2008*
Neal Lipschutz	*2007-present*
Les Hinton	*2008-present*
Gregory Giangrande	*2008-present*
Kenneth Herts	*2008-present*